THE LAWS OF HOSTILITY

THE LAWS
OF HOSTILITY

Politics, Violence, and the Enlightenment

Pierre Saint-Amand

Foreword by Chantal Mouffe

Translated by Jennifer Curtiss Gage

University of Minnesota Press
Minneapolis
London

The University of Minnesota Press gratefully acknowledges financial assistance provided by the French Ministry of Culture for the translation of this book.

Originally published as *Les lois de l'hostilité: La politique à l'âge de Lumières*
Copyright 1992 by Éditions du Seuil.

Published by the University of Minnesota Press
111 Third Avenue South, Suite 290, Minneapolis, MN 55401–2520
Printed in the United States of America on acid-free paper

Library of Congress Cataloging-in-Publication Data

Saint-Amand, Pierre, 1957–
    [Lois de l'hostilité. English]
    The laws of hostility : politics, violence, and the enlightenment /
Pierre Saint-Amand ; foreword by Chantal Mouffe ; translated by
Jennifer Curtiss Gage.
        p.   cm.
    Includes index.
    ISBN 0-8166-2585-9 (alk. paper). — ISBN 0-8166-2586-7 (pbk. : alk. paper)
    1. Political science—France—History—18th century.
    2. Philosophy, French—18th century.   I. Title.
JA84.F8S2513   1996
303.6'01—dc20   96-11840

Contents

Foreword

Chantal Mouffe

Democratic societies are today facing a challenge that they are ill-prepared to meet. Far from having led to a smooth transition to pluralist democracy, the collapse of communism has opened the way to an explosion of ethnic, religious, and nationalistic conflicts that do not make sense to Western liberals. In their view such antagonisms belong to a bygone age, a premodern time when passions had not yet been eliminated by the influence of "sweet commerce" and replaced by the rational dominance of interests and the generalization of "postconventional" identities. Hence the difficulty of democratic thinkers in understanding the current proliferation of particularisms and the new emergence of a variety of supposedly "archaic" antagonisms.

It would be a mistake to see such a situation as a merely temporary problem, soon to be overcome by progress in empirical research. Indeed, it could be argued that it is the very structure of the dominant approach in liberal democratic theory that precludes understanding the present conjuncture. Characterized as it is by rationalism, individualism, and universalism, this type of theory must necessarily remain blind to the nature of the political and to the ineradicability of antagonism. To be sure, the term *political* is increasingly present in liberal philosophy—as the success of so-called political liberalism indicates—but the domain of the political is always approached from an individualistic and rationalist standpoint that reduces it to either economics or ethics. As a consequence the dynamics of the constitution of collective subjects and the crucial role played by passions and antagonisms in this field cannot be grasped. There resides the explanation for the impotence of Western liberals in providing adequate answers to the current problems—an impotence that could have dramatic consequences for the future of democratic institutions.

In order to defend democracy against the various fundamentalisms and to stop the growth of the extreme right, a different approach is urgently needed. To be able to delineate an alternative democratic theory, we first need to discover the reasons for its present shortcomings. This means examining the origins of the modern democratic perspective and revisiting the basic tenets of the Enlightenment.

In *The Laws of Hostility,* Pierre Saint-Amand proposes a political anthropology of the Enlightenment that offers many insights of fundamental importance for such a project. By scrutinizing the writings of Montesquieu, Voltaire, Rousseau, Diderot, and Sade through the perspective developed by René Girard, Saint-Amand brings to the fore the key role played by the logic of *imitation* in their conception of sociability, while at the same time unveiling its repressed dimension. He shows how, in their attempt to ground politics on reason and nature, the *philosophes* of the Enlightenment were led to present an optimistic view of human sociability, seeing violence as an archaic phenomenon that does not really belong to human nature. According to them, antagonistic and violent forms of behavior, everything that is the manifestation of hostility, could be eradicated thanks to the progress of exchange and the development of sociability. Theirs is an idealized view of sociability that acknowledges only one side of what constitutes the dynamics of imitation. Pierre Saint-Amand indicates how in the *Encyclopédie* human reciprocity is envisaged as aiming exclusively at the realization of the good. This is possible because only one part of the mimetic affects, those linked to empathy, are taken into account. However, if one recognizes—following René Girard—the ambivalent nature of the concept of imitation, its antagonistic dimension can be brought to light, and we get a different picture of sociability. The importance of Girard is that he reveals the conflictual nature of mimesis, the double bind by which the same movement that brings human beings together in their common desire for the same objects is also at the origin of their antagonism. Far from being the exterior of exchange, rivalry and violence are therefore its ever-present possibility. Reciprocity and hostility cannot be dissociated, and we have to realize that the social order will always be threatened by violence.

By refusing to acknowledge the antagonistic dimension of imitation, the *philosophes* failed to grasp the complex nature of human reciprocity. They denied the negative side of exchange, its dissociating impulse. This denial was the very condition for the fiction of a social contract from which violence and hostility would have been eliminated and where reciprocity could take the form of a transparent communication among participants. Although in their writings many of them could not completely elude the negative possibilities of imitation, they were unable to formulate its ambivalent character conceptually. It was the very nature of their humanistic project—to ground the autonomy of the social and to secure equality among human beings—that led them to defend an idealized view of human sociability.

The fictitious character of this view, however, was revealed by Sade, who denounced the idea of a social contract and celebrated violence. For Saint-Amand, Sade's view can be seen as a form of aberrant liberalism whose motto could be that private vices work toward the general vice. He cannot be separated from Rousseau, whose idea of a transparent community Sade reproduces in a perverted form: the general will becomes the voluptuous will, and the immediacy of communication becomes the immediacy of debauchery.

I believe that Saint-Amand's critical reading of political anthropology in the Enlightenment has great relevance to our present predicament. The main lesson to be learned from this journey into the beginnings of our modern democratic perspective is that, contrary to what Jürgen Habermas and his followers argue, the epistemological side of the Enlightenment is not to be seen as the precondition for its political side, the democratic project. Far from being the necessary basis for democracy, the rationalist view of human nature, with its denial of the negative aspect of sociability, appears to be its weakest point. By foreclosing the recognition that violence is ineradicable, it renders democratic theory unable to grasp the nature of "the political" and its dimension of hostility and antagonism. The consequence of this blindness to the political is that liberal democratic theory is bound to miss the central task of what we might call "politics," meaning the ensemble of practices, discourses, and institutions that seek to establish an order and organize human coexistence in conditions that are always potentially conflictual because they are affected by the political.

Envisaged from such a viewpoint, politics always involves domesticating hostility and trying to defuse the potential antagonism that exists in human relations. As a consequence, *pace* the rationalists, the central question for democratic politics is not how to arrive at a rational consensus reached without exclusion. In other words, the aim of democracy is not to eliminate passions or to relegate them to the private sphere in order to establish a rational consensus in the public sphere. Rather, it is to tame those passions by mobilizing them toward democratic designs.

Contemporary liberals, far from offering a more adequate view of politics, are in a sense even less willing than their forerunners to acknowledge its dark side. They believe that the development of modern society has definitively established the conditions for a "deliberative democracy" in which decisions on matters of common concern result from the free and unconstrained public deliberation of all. According to liberal theorists, politics in a well-ordered democratic society is the field in which a rational consensus will be established through the free exercise of public reason as in John Rawls, or under the conditions of an undistorted communication as in Habermas. In such a scenario, political actors are presented as rational individuals driven only by their rational self-advantage under the constraints of morality. Passions are erased from the realm of politics, which is reduced to a neutral field of competing interests. By denying the ineradicability of antagonism, this approach forecloses the possibility of acknowledging the political and of grasping the dynamics of its possible forms of emergence. No wonder that, when confronted with the very antagonism that their perspective aims at denying, liberal theorists can only evoke a return to the archaic.

Alas, it is not by denying the violence that is inherent in sociability—violence that no contract can eliminate because it is in fact a component of sociability—that democratic politics can be secured and enhanced. On the contrary, it is by finally acknowledging the contradictory drives set to work by social exchange and the fragility of the democratic order that we will be able to deal more adequately with what the old Kant in one of his more lucid moments designated as our "unsociable sociability."

Introduction

In the view of Ernst Cassirer, Enlightenment thought is inhabited, even obsessed, by a paradox: the question of the origins of humanity. Haunted by its origins, the Enlightenment seems condemned to a process of continual regression with respect to itself. Fundamentally, the question of origins, the problem of establishing law, runs counter to the central project of the Enlightenment—that is, the development of rationalism with a view to progress. More precisely, Cassirer writes that "a fundamental feature of the philosophy of the Enlightenment appears in the fact that, despite its passionate desire for progress, despite its endeavors to break the old tables of the law and to arrive at a new outlook on life, it nevertheless returns again and again to the original problems of humanity."[1] The specter of origins is the skeleton in the closet of Enlightenment political philosophy, the evil spirit that haunts it, the ever-present threat of incompletion.

This book proposes to probe the recesses of the Enlightenment, to expose the crisis of Law that lurks underneath. Indeed, by stripping it of its soothing illusions, we can bring this self-proclaimed Age of Reason closer to us, and perhaps its humanism will speak to our anxieties at last. And ranging somewhat further afield, we might consider this enterprise in the light of Jacques Derrida's more recent general reflections on law as founded upon violence. The law of the future is rooted in violence past. This tension is the key to understanding the double-edged paradox of justice as *Dikè* (justice, right, judgment) and *Eris* (conflict, discord, *polemos*). Inscribed in every process of institution is a phase of violence, often in the form of sacrifice and "uninterpretable" exclusions.[2]

It is this often-overlooked problem that I wish to bring to bear on the consideration of right in the eighteenth century; this is the problem that, gnawing unseen at the very bowels of the social body, insidiously vitiates both the major theoretical advances of the social pact and indeed all forms of political or national organization. But for the political thinkers of the period, it is as if the time of violence is gone forever, as if Enlightened man has embarked on an irreversible process of civilization, a future for which the stage must be cleared; from this point forward, violence can be conceived only as what lies beyond the realm of theory.

This book places the political thought of the Enlightenment under the Machiavellian sign of pathology and suspicion, of original immorality, of an accursed share, an element of evil that pervades communication among men. We must do violence to the Enlightenment in order to correct its transfiguration of the human, to redress the illusory emancipation it claims to confer on mankind.[3]

I will follow the hypothesis of two philosophers who stand apart from the general chorus of pacificist consensus, from the blind idolatry of benevolence and optimistic reciprocity. The first of these philosophers, the Scotsman Adam Ferguson, writes in his *Essay on the History of Civil Society:* "Mankind not only find in their condition the sources of variance and dissension; they appear to have in their minds the seeds of animosity, and to embrace the occasions of mutual opposition, with alacrity and pleasure."[4] He concludes: "Thus in treating of human affairs, we would draw every consequence from a principle of union, or a principle of dissension" (Section III, 16).

The second is Simon-Nicolas-Henri Linguet, who in 1767 wrote *Théorie des lois civiles* (Theory of civil laws) in which he refutes the *philosophes'* enterprise of idealization as an exercise in flattery that gilds over origins, deceptively substituting one history for another. For Linguet, society is born of blood, in the submission of farmers to gangs of soldiers. At the origin is no contract of goodwill and of mutual help, no shared needs, but rather violence and force:

> Other writers, more comfortable with calm, cannot imagine that battle cries or the clash of weapons could have marred the birth of the world. They endeavor to banish such an inhuman roar from the cradle of society. They desire this institution to be the result of free and unanimous consent, but it repulses them to see it being born amidst commotion and delivered by soldiers; it pleases them to suppose that it is the product of the mild-mannered relationships of agriculture and trade. They would prefer that plowshares, rather than swords, be the basis for first governments, and they would have laws fashioned by the calloused hands of Laborers, rather than the bloody hands of Heroes.[5]

Repeating Linguet's gesture, I would like to show that the *philosophes* cloaked the origins of society in a veil of modesty, refusing to consider human beings as they really are. Oddly enough, they aspired to be the saviors of mankind, but to do so they had to sever human beings from their own evil. In so doing, they produced irresponsible concepts. For their naive optimism, for glossing over human complexity, their humanism deserves to be repudiated. Enlightenment speculation into origins serves to create a distance between man's past and his future in the epiphany of the law, between humankind's first links with the sacred and its move into social faith. I want to show that the origins remain a threatening palimpsest over which the *philosophes'* positive theory is inscribed and that the modern order is invaded by the archaic, the barbaric. Enlightenment thought is built on the shaky foundation of primitive violence.

We must ask ourselves how the *philosophes* could have been at once so close to and yet so far from understanding violence. Where does this force of negation, this foreclosure, this capacity to neutralize violence come from? In my view, their denial is contemporary with the collapse of all forms of transcendence (God, the King). As soon as reponsibility for founding society came to rest on human shoulders, as soon as it was possible to conceive man's future in terms of horizontal, egalitarian relations, that is to say, in the perspective of social *autonomy*, the eighteenth century found itself confronted with a new social economy. And hence it boasted of optimism and good faith, by endowing man, its philosophical creature, with ideal qualities.[6]

The *philosophes* needed a being who was up to the demands of a future both glorious and realizable. The violence of relations, the bewildering antagonism between human beings, could only be relegated to a long-ago past. *Exit* hostility. The new age of the republic and of History will paint a benevolent face on humankind. Man will rediscover his "nature." Contemporary law, waiting to be codified, will be full of goodwill. Natural human goodness will provide the cornerstone for a new concept of justice. At last, the moment for mutual contract had arrived, built on a foundation of reason, goodwill, and public interest. The time for war was over, along with its attendant evils: vendettas, assassinations, duels, battles of honor, reprisals. An entire system of justice was found to be obsolete. Peter Gay analyzed this as the invention of a "politics of decency."[7] He recalls the cheerful optimism of Constance, a character in Denis Diderot's play *Le Fils naturel:* "The time of barbarism is past. The century has become enlightened. Reason has grown refined, and the nation's books are filled with its precepts. The books that inspire benevolence in men are practically the only ones read."[8]

This certainly describes the project of the Revolutionaries of 1789, the practical heirs to the *philosophes,* who conceived of violence as an unfortunate digression from the history of humankind. Fortunately, thanks to them, a return to nature had become possible: man will rediscover that he is essentially virtuous. Saint-Just, at last giving a direction and a meaning to human destiny, writes that "the human heart advances from nature to violence, from violence to morality."[9] The Terror was to come as an unforeseeable surprise to all these well-meaning lawyers, as an unambiguous error attributable to ancient institutions, as slag from the arbitrary past. How indeed could they explain the new outbreak of violence? What basis could they find for it?[10]

Imitation

This book should be read in light of a concept that is central to the eighteenth-century *philosophes'* definitions of society: imitation. Imitation is the motor, the affective drive par excellence of sociability. The *Encyclopédie* article "Society" defines imitation as that which makes social exchange possible. Imitation propels human beings toward their neighbors. The mimetic impulse is responsible for initiating social contact through effects of sympathy and pity, and the desire to gather together.[11] But from here the *Encyclopédie* goes on to formulate an ideal concept of sociability. It consequently envisages human reciprocity as essentially directed toward the good. A natural inclination inspires us to seek out the company of others and leads us to want to share our happiness with them: sociability, we read in the *Encyclopédie*, "is that disposition that inspires us to do unto others all the good that is within our power, to fashion our happiness according to others' happiness, and always to subordinate our private gain to the general, common gain."[12]

Not until Jean-Jacques Rousseau arrives with his version of Platonism does the concept of imitation begin to reveal its ambivalent character. Rousseau rightfully discerns the vicious tendency that lurks within the evil genius of imitation, its constitutive *difference*. Imitation in Rousseau becomes oblivious to its own erstwhile nature. The imitative reply, originally well meaning, now incites rivalry and competition. Imitation takes on the lineaments of conflict, as if the parties involved were possessed by it. Rousseau attempts to repudiate this negative imitation by trying to efface the other-as-obstacle, by avoiding the chiasmus of a reciprocal gaze. His myth of constituent individualism is a by-product of this attempt.

The schizophrenic nature of imitation, its inherent double bind, suggests an approach that is broadly applicable to the entire period. Beginning with a positive conception of imitation, the *philosophes* are somehow quite capable of ignoring the fact that the same imitation can be responsible for antagonistic behavior. Imitation as a principle of identity between desires leads people to desire the same objects, but in this very movement toward each other, imitation can separate through aggravated acts of competition. Imitation can no longer be understood solely as a formative and generating force in the way it activates the social bond. It also constitutes an equally negative force of disintegration.

I would introduce the term *reciprocity* in order to add structural breadth to the concept of imitation and to account for its morphogenetic manifestations. The term *reciprocity* embraces a complex series of behavior patterns, generally describing human interactions including the most fatal ones. Although Enlightenment philosophers have an idealized view of reciprocity as a transparent act of communication between one subject and another, their writings illustrate its negative possibilities for transformation and complexity. Reciprocity thus mutates into rivalrous strategies; it evolves into competition; it feeds on violence. Reciprocity couples with the ambivalence of imitation, even in its most destabilizing forms.

I would like to offer examples of the numerous violent encounters that constitute exchange—the crossed wires of relations, the risks of reciprocity. Uppermost in my mind are struggles for prestige, the passion for recognition, all the permutations of mimetic rivalry. In spite of the difficulty of conceptualizing violent negativity, in spite of its unthinkability, it must be understood as inherent to the possibility of social order, and even as a permanent temptation. Violence cannot be relegated to distant myths, to an Oriental desert, or, as in Voltaire, to a time before the advent of great History. Violence is not a novelty belonging to the civil state, a shocking lapse into barbarity that takes humankind by surprise. It is not a loss of human nature; on the contrary, it is the fabric of our complex origins.

A philosophy of right flounders when confronted by the kind of behavior that the Enlightenment believed to be nontheorizable. All forms of violence—as the inverse of a reasoned social contract—belong to this unthinkable theoretical space. Vengeance, for example, is one of the forms of irrational social behavior that Enlightenment philosophy tried to relegate to a prehistory that no longer concerned it. Vengeance represents a model of reciprocity that the Enlightenment refuses to consider. It is thought of as an aberration. According to the *Encyclopédie*, vengeance—defined quite simply as the opposite of sociability—"destroys the very principle of benevolence, replacing it with a sentiment of hatred and animosity. It is vicious on its own, contrary to the public good, and natural law formally condemns it."[13] Vengeance does not belong to the social economy. It is unnatural. It is scandalous in its very form; it is conceptually corrupt.

As a form of response to the other, vengeance as retaliation falls, curiously, within the treacherous logic of the gift. An antagonistic form of the gift, vengeance is a relation of hateful obligation, a dangerous debt. In vengeance the desire for recognition, the symbolic foundation of the gift, is exaggerated to the point of delirium. Vengeance institutes a relation of malevolent reversibility, of spiteful reciprocity between individuals. *Lex talionis*, the law of the talion, is the diametric opposite of the contract: it goes to the extreme of singling out the partners in exchange, rather than universalizing them. In this the talion is the obverse of the contract that transcendentalizes and exteriorizes ad infinitum the object of exchange.

We shall see how vengeance arises out of the prehistory of law, however, to haunt the most optimistic formulations of the *philosophes*. The threat of the resurgent past hinges on the false conception that these thinkers have of violence, which must always be excluded from the social, like an impure element. Appearing as an aberration in the dawning of the civil state, violence is not considered to belong to human nature. This is how Baron de Montesquieu maintains the purity of the state of nature. For him, presocial man is weak and a stranger to aggression, yet he is haunted by a fear of the other. Rousseau later points out the contradiction contained in this premise. Fear can only be fear of aggression, says Rousseau, forcing us to view aggressive confrontation as originary. Rousseau formulates the most radical objection to the Hobbesian hypothesis of perpetual war in the state of nature:

> If this mutual and destructive enmity were a part of our constitution, it would thus still make itself felt and would repel us in spite of ourselves, pervading all social bonds. Humanity's terrible hate would gnaw away at the heart of man. We would be afflicted by the birth of our own children; we would rejoice at the death of our brethren, and should we happen upon someone sleeping, our first impulse would be to kill them.[14]

Montesquieu and Rousseau push vengeance back into prehistory; they seek forms of exchange, of relation, that are exempt from the violence of our origins. For Montesquieu, commercial trade would make us hospitable in spite of ourselves, while for Rousseau, the ideal civil state would be one in which forms of reciprocity are restricted to a minimum. In contrast, what structures the network of relations in Diderot and the Marquis de Sade is revenge in its subtlest forms. For these two, the present recalls the shameful past; the law of the talion casts its shadow over the contract.

Exchange and Hostility

In an attempt to reestablish the sense of danger inherent in exchange, the fragile equilibrium of cultures, this book draws on several approaches. These include that of Marcel Mauss, who understood the troubling paradox of the gift—the obligation to pay it back, and also in the background, Thorstein Veblen's and Raymond Aron's sociology, Michel Serres's anthropological works, and Jean-Pierre Dupuy's research in economics. But above all I invoke René Girard's theory of mimetic desire, which, in my opinion, offers concepts that come closest to capturing the complex phenomenon of rivalry.

Girard's anthropology does not provide this book with specific tools of analysis but, rather, defines the horizon of destabilizing elements that imitation assumes in the texts we are about to study. His anthropology permits us to address the unconscious or implicit portion of the positive concepts of Enlightenment social theory. If recourse to Girard affords us any theoretical advantage, it is because his theory works on two levels. For Girard, the concept of imitation can be considered only through its principle of ambivalence; it operates fundamentally as a double bind. This is what makes Girard's work such a radical departure from thought on mimesis since Plato: the nature of mimesis is studied in its aspect of conflict, as mimesis of appropriation (rivalry over the same object) rather than as mimesis of propriation (adequation, resemblance to a model). As for reciprocity, for Girard it is the result of the violent relation with the other, and no longer what maintains exchange, what makes exchange possible. For Girard, exchange always goes against reciprocity; it leaves reciprocity behind it as its dangerous flip side. Reciprocity's sudden crazes, the way it brings mimetic interferences to a head, lead to processes of undifferentiation, to a collapse of hierarchies, to forms of social desymbolization. The silence maintained around the antagonistic dimension of imitation represents a scandal that Girard's theory relentlessly attempts to denounce. He views this silence as a veritable historic mutilation, a deliberate blind spot that flatters our

superior sense of humanity while preventing us from consider-
ing the fragility of our societies and the violence that threatens
them.[15] We stand therefore in marked opposition to Claude Lévi-
Strauss's anthropology, in order to espouse Pierre Clastres's criticism of Lévi-Strauss's system, which he analyzes as modeled
exclusively on the basis of exchange and sociability. Lévi-Strauss
fails to take violence into account: he banishes it outside the
group and makes it an inadmissible property of the social. Clastres's objection to Lévi-Strauss is encapsulated in the following
formula: "To be mistaken about violence . . . is to be mistaken
about society."[16]

Indeed, Clastres observes that Lévi-Strauss pays minimal attention to the phenomenon of war in primitive society, almost to the
point of suppressing violence. According to Clastres, Lévi-Strauss
accords exchange a kind of ontological priority over war. It is
exchange that is original and positive; war is considered only in a
negative light. For Lévi-Strauss, the primitive society's fundamental desire is for exchange. Clastres elaborates: "War, a derail-
ment or rupture of the movement toward exchange, can represent
[for Lévi-Strauss] only the nonessence, the nonbeing of society. . . .
It is an accidental property, inessential, aleatory."[17] In this view
Lévi-Strauss's anthropology is taken to be the exact obverse of
that of Thomas Hobbes, for primitive society is articulated as
based on reciprocal exchange rather than on reciprocal conflict.
Friendship takes the place of hostility.

In opposition to Lévi-Strauss, Clastres develops the idea that
generalized friendship does not accurately portray the primitive
society. To this effect he finds two powerful arguments: (1) the
communities' desire to remain autonomous and independent and
(2) their desire to affirm their difference, their nonidentification
with one another. Clastres goes so far as to reverse Lévi-Strauss's
proposition: war is no longer the unfortunate outcome of unsuc-
cessful exchange; it is, rather, exchange that becomes the tactical
outcome of war. Convincingly, alliance as *strategy* is shown as
the mediator between war and exchange.

Claude Lefort criticizes Lévi-Strauss on the same point, re-
proaching him for having avoided true human behavior—the real-

ity of struggle between human beings—by being blind to the antithetical character of exchange. Lévi-Strauss's work, says Lefort, consists of a purely mathematical retreat that substitutes "an *ideated* exchange for a *lived* exchange, for the experience of rivalry, prestige, or love."[18] Human beings are sacrificed for the benefit of symbols; life becomes an imposing system. Cycles of reciprocity become a veritable potlatch of abstract signs in Lévi-Strauss's work. The ethnologist seems to have missed the elementary structures of rivalry.

The Lineage of Strife

This book begins with Montesquieu and ends with Sade—an odd itinerary, one might think, for political theory. It moves from pure theory to political fictions, to politics as fiction. My point is to show the disintegration that affects certain concepts over the course of the century, to expose their complex inner and interworkings. As manners and morals begin to decay, concepts tend to take on a more negative energy and acquire an even more ambivalent density: the social sphere is delivered up to the war of concepts. Speculation on origins becomes an opportunity for the *philosophes* to cast accusations and to refute all sorts of allegations. We enter into the great intellectual battle of the century: intellectuals vying to proclaim that humans are originally good or originally savage. Hobbes, at the center of the fracas, appears as an innocent bystander; he even becomes the scapegoat of conflicting theories. The aged ancestor abandons the coveted object of theoretical investigation to the younger generation. This is the Hobbesian concept that is most often refuted: the notion of original violence, a premise that ends up provoking the most unruly passions. Violence contradicts violence: this is the new science of law.

The creative energy of the theoreticians is inconceivable outside the clamorous context of rivalry. And in spite of the relative autonomy accorded to the anthropological system of each author, the present book is, in the most rigorous sense of the term, a *comparative* politics. Montesquieu, who gives the impression of having created his system from start to finish, stands as the absolute model of political science. And consequently, he attracts all sorts of rivals throughout the century. New, alternative theories had to begin by refuting his monumental text. Because of his exclusionary move, because of the almost prophetic distance he maintained, he created an infinite space for rivals: he abandoned the subject to the jealous brothers of the horde. The most envious attack came from Rousseau in *Emile:* "The only modern in a position to create this great and useless science [the science of political right] was the illustrious Montesquieu."[19] As for the discipline's ancestors, they are quickly cut down to size by Rousseau's sharp wit: Hugo Grotius is "a child of bad faith"; "Hobbes bases himself on sophisms" (458). Rousseau should know, as he is the one who believes that philosophy is not a search for truth but a persuasive juxtaposition of contradictory systems and theories: "The essential thing," he writes, "is to think differently from others" (269). Voltaire, in the same jealous spirit, also attacks the revered names of political theory: Hobbes, Grotius, and Montesquieu. Annoyed by their celebrated status, he disposes of them with a single introductory quip: "Grotius is frankly a pedant, Hobbes a sad philosopher, and Montesquieu a wit."[20] Diderot says it better than anyone else, exposing to view the subject's rotten underbelly: "People have concocted all sorts of origins for society: a fine topic for the kind of birds that grow fat in the fog, the ones they call metaphysicians. . . . Since everyone dreams as he pleases on this subject, no one will object if I, too, dream."[21] Law is no longer attributed to transcendent principles such as God. It becomes inscribed in a network of debts and influences, allowing each theoretician's own formulation in the midst of competing systems.

The same goes for *epistemes,* which should not be regarded as zones of homogeneous discourses, as Michel Foucault defined them.[22] They are quite capable of generating their own internal contradictions. Communication between intellectuals is necessarily polemical. The similarity of matter under discussion provokes a desire to establish differences, to turn propositions around at will. Communication does not correspond to Habermas's utopia. It does not always converge toward harmonious consensus; it does not necessarily gain access to truth.[23] On the contrary, communication creates more and more systems of contradictions and irreconcilable propositions. In other words, rationality is rare. Every *episteme* is saturated with competition and creates a network that is charged with problematization. Toward the end of the century, Kant described civil peace for citizens, but none for philosophy; rather, for him war keeps apathy at bay and reason awake. This, then, is the philosopher's command: "One of the benevolent and wise dispositions of nature" is the propensity or impulse to "*battle* to promote one's philosophy and . . . gathered in masses into opposing camps (school versus school, as army takes on army), to *wage open warfare.*"[24]

For Reinhart Koselleck, this energetic debate, this competition of theoretical models, represents the most scandalously hypocritical aspect of the *philosophes:* their critique of politics is devoid of any effort to mobilize action in the domain of real politics. In its eagerness to triumph, theory departs from reality. The *philosophes* declare themselves partisans of morality, which they impose as the absolute perspective. But they end up with unequaled political pretensions. Before long they want to pass for the true masters of the nation; they invent a rival authority, a new sovereignty. The philosopher-critic becomes the "king of kings, the true sovereign."[25] This exacerbated controversy over political notions culminates in the Revolution, which stakes the most triumphant claim to this newly announced sovereignty.

Alexis de Tocqueville had already brilliantly anticipated Koselleck when, in *The Old Regime and the French Revolution,* he noted the *philosophes'* remarkable bid to seize power. This coup d'état is all the more astonishing to Tocqueville because it seems to derive from a purely theoretical and abstract obsession with social questions. The *philosophes* are politically removed from the world of politics, yet they remain captivated by political thinking. It was this lack of vision, this incredible distance from the busy world of politics—this invisibility—that, according to Tocqueville, exercised the writers' theoretical imaginations and contributed to making their ideas so daring: "Questions such as the origin of human society, its earliest forms, the original rights of citizens and of authority, the 'natural' and the 'artificial' relations between men, of the legitimacy of custom, and even the whole conception of law—all these bulked large in the literature of the day."[26] Tocqueville also points out how much the game of contradiction animated this new theoretical endeavor: "The political programs advocated by our eighteenth-century writers varied so much that any attempt to synthesize them or deduce a single coherent theory of government from them would be labor lost" (139). Tocqueville then asks how this "passion" for politics came to be transferred to the masses. The answer, according to him, is not hard to find. Theory simply found itself on fertile ground; the very process of social transformation, the desire for novelty, unleashed an irreversible momentum. But the greatest lure was the speculative seduction of systems. That was what won the crowd over and swayed it to the universality of revolutionary desire: "The philosopher's cloak provided safe cover for the passions of the day" (142). Political contagion began by being transmitted through words: "Even the politicians' phraseology was borrowed largely from the books they read; it was cluttered up with abstract words, gaudy flowers of speech, sonorous clichés, and literary turns of phrase" (147).

Decadence

One of the mechanisms I examine in the present study is the way the political side of things was taken over and harnessed by the world of morals and manners. Nevertheless, we shall see that in this gush of words, in this effusion of political language, critical claims renounced their pretensions to idealism and foundered in their own negativity. The Age of Enlightenment, from Montesquieu and Rousseau to Diderot and Sade, bore witness to this transformation. Our study inevitably follows the same process whereby mores were investigated increasingly as *culture.* Manners declined. Their decadence was part of the destruction of everything that makes society possible. This is how I interpret a certain conceptual squandering of the objects of exchange and a similar attack on those who were perceived as the models of manners. Culture revolted against the past; ancestors were damned. The nation no longer needed fathers because it had its sons.

Enlightenment thinkers attempted to invent the most transparent social contracts; they truly desired a responsible, reciprocal social bond. The *philosophes* sought to found politics on reason and nature at the same time. But it would seem that their works could never reach this desired origin. By dismantling all the great social foundations, religious and mythic, they ended up producing simulations of the very foundations they had rejected—

political seductions, spectacularly staged patriotic shows, social rites. This is why we must deconstruct the great political narratives created in the Age of Voltaire. These contaminated forms, these games of political mimicry no longer depict the obscene inverse of the political, its inadmissible representation; on the contrary, they become its inherent preconditions. Montesquieu's Usbek and Voltaire's Mahomet, carried away by the heady fumes of religion, are undoubtedly negative figures. They readily bring to mind our modern demonization of the Ayatollah Khomeini and Saddam Hussein, for example. And in his benevolent beatitude Zadig, the prince of reason, is not far removed from our political impostors. Rousseau's and Voltaire's political foundations seek their legitimacy by reverting to religious rites; Sade's republic requires ceremonies. Further, the political works themselves insist on assuming a sacred quality in their attempt to be foundational, initiatory. The *philosophes* may be disguised as inspired legislators, but beneath this travesty they are men of miracles at heart.

Perhaps a few will find this vision of the Age of Voltaire somewhat strange and discomfiting. This is precisely the effect I am aiming for. What will emerge is a century much closer to its fears, constantly brushing up against the risks that are inherent in social relations. This book shatters the *philosophes'* optimism, sacrifices it, one might say, to the advantage of the violent relations that haunt humankind.

The view of the eighteenth century that I offer is at once archaic and haunted by its unfulfilled future, by the social difficulty of maturation. It shows human beings tied to their dangerous past, which is also their present. It admits the emancipation of the citizen only by invoking passionate frenzies: rivalries, sacrificial exclusions, violent contagions, delirious envy. This book accepts the complex and confused destiny of social interaction. Morality, as I see it, is not the path that will lead us to an ideal of humankind, to a nature released from the bondage of its forced alienation. Morality begins, rather, from a point of fearful recognition.

1 / Political Prejudice
(Montesquieu)

Montesquieu confided that he had composed *The Spirit of the Laws* with the attentiveness of an artist: "Et moi aussi je suis peintre" (I, too, am a painter). Not daunted by the encyclopedic nature of the work (the diversity of nations, laws, and manners), nor by the time it consumed (twenty years, the better part of a lifetime), he finally felt, in 1748, that he had captured the essence of this majestic subject. The formal perfection of *The Spirit of the Laws* has often been pointed out, along with its scientific rigor: Montesquieu is cast as the Newton of political theory. There remain, however, some shadowy areas in this work. It is as if the complexities he had tried to expunge keep reappearing in the interstices. Montesquieu hesitates between "the real life of men" and his aim of applying the scientific method. There is a conflict between the work's attempt at formalization (typology) and its object (people and nations). It might be said that Montesquieu struggled between the spirit of laws and the spirit of human beings. Beyond the concept of "principle," which he forged as the most rational category for the description of governments, a whole series of less well-defined concepts are differentiated.

One of these concepts is that of manners. It appears in book XIX of *The Spirit of the Laws*, long after the rigorous premises of the first books. Montesquieu experts agree on the uniquely important place this book holds in the work,[1] but reverting to the conflict between moral and physical causes, they invoke reasons that are not altogether convincing. Manners are the general spirit of a nation, a form of natural cohesion among people: "Laws are established, manners are inspired; these proceed from a general spirit, those from a particular institution: now it is as dangerous, nay more so, to subvert the general spirit as to change a particular institution."[2] Before constructing his positive theory, Montesquieu must first grapple with the earlier dimension that is humankind's original sociability.

Describing the difficulty of his enterprise in the preface to *The Spirit of the Laws*, Montesquieu depicts human nature in terms that convey the crucial importance of the notion of manners. He proposes the following definition of man as a mimetic creature: "Man, that flexible being, conforming in society to the thoughts and impressions of others, is equally capable of knowing his own nature whenever it is laid open to his view, and of losing the very sense of it when this idea is banished from his mind" (xxxiii). Manners are the generalized expression of the human animal. Montesquieu thus offers this definition of the general spirit: "Mankind are influenced by various causes: by the climate, by the religion, by the laws, by the maxims of government, by precedents, morals, and customs; whence is formed a general spirit of nations" (XIX, 4, 293). Nations seem to be governed by two types of mediation, of cohesive forces: one type that is external and transcendental (religion, things of the past) and one that is internal (morals, manners). In the first instance, group identification finds its justification in the invention of a model that is outside the human sphere; in the second, human reciprocity produces its own models of behavior through interaction. The ideal government would be one able to strike a balance between laws, morals, and manners. When laws are in violent opposition to customs, to the general spirit of a nation, revolt inevitably ensues:

> In all societies, which are nothing but unity in spirit, a common character is formed. This universal soul assumes a manner of thinking that is the effect of a chain of infinite causes, which multiply and combine over the centuries. Once the tone is set and received, it

alone governs, and all that sovereigns, magistrates, and peoples may do or imagine, whether they would flout this tone or conform to it, relates to it, and it reigns even to the point of total destruction.[3]

Perched at this fragile intersection of laws, morals, and manners is the legislator, along with Montesquieu himself, no doubt, as he writes *The Spirit of the Laws*. Montesquieu sets out to apportion their due, respectively, to the political unconscious that drives people and to the laws that ought to enlighten them. The primary goal of science would be to desubjectivize the function of the legislator, to remove him from the selfish realm of passions and self-interest. Science should also aim to desacralize this function by stripping the legislator of any divine inspiration or revelation.

But underneath this process of secularization, Montesquieu himself fabricates a subtler, and perhaps even more essential, resacralization, which lies in the aesthetic value he attributes to the labor of conceiving *The Spirit of the Laws*. The work's success is taken as a resurrection, a triumph over the world of shadows alluded to in his preface: "Often have I begun, and as often have I laid aside, this undertaking. I have a thousand times given the leaves I had written to the winds" (lxix). The book's epigraph alludes to its mythical birth: *prolem sine matre creatum*, "a child born of no mother." Behind the book's claim of originality is a clear bid for sacralization, bolstered by the special status the author is quickly accorded among his fellow human beings. *The Spirit of the Laws* is a *pharmakos*, a remedy capable of curing the world of its impurities: "The most happy of mortals should I think myself could I contribute to make mankind recover from their prejudices" (lxviii).

In his eulogy to Montesquieu, d'Alembert recalls the voluntary expatriation the author imposed on himself in order to write his book: "Thus he rose by degrees to the most noble title that a wise man may merit, that of legislator of nations."[4] Because Montesquieu had virtually given up his life for this work, d'Alembert hoped to see "*The Spirit of the Laws* placed upon his coffin" during the funeral ceremony dedicated to its author by the French Academy (78). Thus the phantasm of the political writer that was created around Montesquieu was doubled by the phantasm of the sacrificial legislator: the truth of the work and the soundness of laws could be attained only at the price of a truly exhaustive meditation, of a life sacrificed. Montesquieu himself was to be rewarded for his titanic effort; no one has better expressed this debt shared by all historians than Georg Wilhelm Friedrich Hegel, who spoke of his predecessor's "immortal work."[5]

The Evil Spirit of the Laws

Montesquieu's scientific ambition grew out of his feeling that, behind the variety of human types, their manners, and laws, there must be a structure capable of accounting for their specificity, their singularity: "I have first of all considered mankind, and the result of my thoughts has been, that amidst such an infinite diversity of laws and manners, they were not solely conducted by the caprice of fancy" (lxvii). But he soon discovered that people were led by their prejudices (their unconsciousness in relation to the self, a dimension that *The Spirit of the Laws* hopes to cure) and above all by their passions. Recent critics of Montesquieu often use the term *desire* over *passion*. But only in the case of despotism does this substitution make sense. This has to do, I believe, with the theory that underlies their definition of desire: for this essentially Freudian theory, despotic passion is desire in its purest form. It represents the all-powerful—and narcissistic— force of desire. I would like to show that the theory of mimetic desire makes possible a fuller analysis of Montesquieu's work; it also more successfully identifies the unique passion or desire that is particular to each of the governments he studied. The principle of each one is bound to a passion that is consubstantial with it.

In fact, it is possible to say that the entire formal organization of Montesquieu's essay hinges on the mimetic dimension. The concept of relation—which is central to his definition of laws and which he defines in the narrowest and yet most general of terms— mimics on a theoretical level the human relations within the groups he later describes. We read one after the other: "Laws . . . are the necessary relations arising from the nature of things" (I, 1, 1); the spirit of the laws "consists in the various relations which the laws may bear to different objects" (I, 3, 7). Montesquieu's entire theoretical apparatus rests on the equivalent notion of reciprocity. Raymond Aron, in *Main Currents in Sociological Thought*, was perhaps the first person to underscore this point. More recently,

Tzvetan Todorov has observed that Montesquieu organizes the social according to "relations of reciprocity" and "relations of subordination"—"symmetrical and asymmetrical relations."[6] Alain Grosrichard defines the principle of government as a relation of reciprocity, a relation of commandment and obedience.[7] Herein lies the most startling aspect of modernity in Montesquieu's socioanthropology. The political is rid of any metaphysics: nothing is left but relations of power.

Relation or reciprocity is originary in Montesquieu. It is coextensive with the individual. Any definition of the law must take this reality into account: "Before there were intelligent beings, they were possible; they had therefore possible relations, and consequently possible laws. Before laws were made, there were relations of possible justice" (I, 1, 2). This is what enables Montesquieu to bring out the structural specificity of each government and its particular way of defining the exercise of power. Even within each government, Montesquieu establishes a politics of relations. While successfully uncovering their structural character, he recognizes the reversibility of these relations. This is what renders governments fragile; it is what makes possible their transformation and corruption, which Hannah Arendt also observed.[8] Montesquieu is less concerned with the "nature" of government than with the relations that define it, with the interactions that constitute its dynamics—what Montesquieu will call the "principle" of government, that is, "the human passions which set it in motion" (III, 1, 19).

The Democratic Extreme

Let us begin with democracy. Its principle is virtue, which Montesquieu defines as self-denial for the love of the public good. Virtue also means the mastery of ambition, a passion that, located by Montesquieu in the individual, designates the preference for oneself to others, whence the following pronouncement: "The love of equality in a democracy limits ambition to the sole desire, to the sole happiness, of doing greater services to our country than the rest of our fellow-citizens" (V, 3, 41). Otherwise, anarchy ensues, with everyone pitted against everyone else; the common good is forgotten and rivalry rules the people: "The objects of their desires are changed," writes Montesquieu (III, 3, 21). Selfish energy is not channeled toward the same goal, nor are individual interests transcended. On the contrary, the most obvious forms of violent reciprocity take hold among people: "Formerly the wealth of individuals constituted the public treasure; but now this has become the patrimony of private persons. The members of the commonwealth riot on the public spoils, and its strength is only the power of a few, and the license of many" (III, 3, 21).

What Montesquieu does not say is that the fragility of democracy stems from the very principle that constitutes it: equality. Equality ought to embody a balanced reciprocity of relations. In *The Spirit of the Laws*, the failure of democracy issues from the very excess of equality. Indeed, democracy makes its citizens doubles of one another. Immediate violence arises from the transformation of reciprocity into forms of rivalry:

> The principle of democracy is corrupted . . . when they [the people] fall into a spirit of extreme equality, and when each citizen would fain be upon a level with those whom he has chosen to command him. Then the people, incapable of bearing the very power they have delegated, want to manage everything themselves, to debate for the senate, to execute for the magistrate, and to decide for the judges. (VIII, 2, 109)

The chapter on the corruption of the principle of democracy paints a vivid tableau of this social disarray, of the "license" that destroys democracy. Here we encounter all the figures of undifferentiation; a sort of libertinism pervades all aspects of the social. Selfishness overtakes one and all, with the reciprocal arousal of self-interest (*amour de soi*) and the universal display of narcissism. All hierarchies are abandoned: "We find in Xenophon's *Banquet* a very lively description of a republic in which the people abused their equality. Each guest gives in his turn the reason why he is satisfied" (VIII, 2, 109). Between the extreme spirit of equality and the moderated spirit of equality, Montesquieu seeks to place a conceptual abyss, a clear structural difference: "As distant as heaven is from earth, so is the true spirit of equality from that of extreme equality" (VIII, 3, 111). Yet he fails to see the paradox that inheres in the principle of equality itself, such that equality contains the cause of its own downfall. He is intent upon establishing a complicated reciprocity of commandment and obedience:

one must both obey and command one's equals. "The true spirit of equality" implies that one's masters "should be none but [one's] equals" (VIII, 3, 111). Montesquieu multiplies the specular mechanisms at work in democracy: everyone is master and subject, subject and master; everyone commands and obeys, in situations of constant reversibility.

Even more remarkably, it is the very success of democracy that leads to its ruin, through none other than people's jealousy of the democratic apparatus itself. A sort of generalized narcissism that is generated within the group proves fatal to it. The very people who are set apart and kept at a distance in order to govern, who are supposed to represent the group as models of their rights, end up becoming objects of envy. This delegation of their own power is precisely what the people can no longer tolerate. They become possessed by equality: "Great success, especially when chiefly owing to the people, intoxicates them to such a degree that it is impossible to contain them within bounds. Jealous of their magistrates, they soon become jealous likewise of the magistracy; enemies to those who govern, they soon prove enemies also to the constitution" (VIII, 4, 112).

Montesquieu acknowledges elsewhere that democratic virtue cannot occur without extraordinary sublimation on the part of individuals. Virtue presupposes a nearly monastic asceticism for him. Effective only if desire is denied, virtue is, essentially, privation. Democratic virtue is nourished by a genuine sacrifice of self: "The less we are able to satisfy our private passions, the more we abandon ourselves to those of a general nature" (V, 2, 40). The way democracy functions can be understood only through an examination of the narrowly reciprocal relations it requires. If democratic citizens are not all despots, it is because they share a common submission to the despotism of the law. Reciprocal obedience to the law, their passion for the law, which is moreover their torment, spares them from reciprocal violence. If they submit to their fellow citizens, it is because they have all submitted to the authority of the laws. Only obedience to the laws—that celestial sphere onto which men cast all their selfish frustrations—can deliver them: thus is Rousseau's general will expressed. It, too, requires that individual interests be converted to the collective duty. In his analysis of Montesquieu, Louis Althusser recognized this as the ultimate metaphysical dilemma of democracy: "In democracy, the men who are 'everything' are nonetheless not at the mercy of their own caprice. The citizens are not so many despots. Their omnipotence subordinates them to a political structure which they recognize and which transcend[s] them as individual men: the order of the laws."[9] Democracy has found its Leviathan.

It is not only this necessary self-denial that maintains democracy, the narcissism of the self giving way to the more powerful narcissism that is love of country; the government's health is manifested not only in the citizens' reciprocity with respect to the law, but also in a relation that predates the advent of the citizen. The models of democratic virtue are the nation's sages, the fathers themselves who have interiorized the law. These are the moral tutors, the models of desire for the sons, whose role is to imitate the passions of their ancestors.

Here we come to an internal contradiction in Montesquieu's argument that Althusser seems delighted to unearth and that serves as proof that the baron never wished for a republic. Althusser notices that Montesquieu establishes a surprising division within democracy, as if there were "two peoples within the people."[10] Montesquieu does indeed bring back division and hierarchy. What fuels this separation, once again, is emulative mediation, or mimetic desire. Montesquieu must provide the people with models in the form of dignitaries and magistrates. What Althusser the Marxist sees as a return to social division and hierarchy, we should read as mimetic competition, specular obligation. Raymond Aron understood this, observing that Montesquieu's sociology could not do without the concept of rivalry.

Montesquieu founded the stability of democracy upon the love of frugality. He defines this love as follows: "Since every individual ought here to enjoy the same happiness and the same advantages, they should consequently taste the same pleasures and form the same hopes, which cannot be expected but from a general frugality" (V, 3, 41). In order to maintain the democratic balance, Montesquieu is obliged to construe the "desire to have" as perfectly mastered or inhibited, as not participating in the universe of competition—not arising from envy for what the other possesses—but, rather, limited to the sphere of personal and domestic needs: "The love of frugality limits the *desire of having* to the study of procuring necessaries to our family" (V, 3, 41; emphasis added). In other words, frugality is the mastery of desire and competitive libido. It guards against the obscene avidity of private interests. We read further: "Neither is it those who *envy* or admire the luxury of the great [who are fond of a frugal life]" (V, 4, 42; emphasis added). The dilemma of democracy is clear: how is distinction to be overcome? Montesquieu is forced to create artificial theoretical conditions in order for democracy to exist and for equality to triumph. In order to subdue the competitive instinct, the instinct for mimetic rivalry, which provokes a desire for what the other possesses (for what the other desires); in order quite simply to keep democratic society from becoming envy-ridden, Montesquieu proposes a series of laws: he suggests the equal allotment of lands and the regulation of dowries, settlements, and inheritances so that wealth will be equitably distributed. He will be the first, alas, to admit the idealistic nature of his measures.

Monarchy: The Place of Honor

The monarchical principle, more than any other, is incapable of escaping the logic of mimetic desire. Honor operates through preferences and distinctions; it differentiates by nature. Montesquieu considers ambition to be inherently present in honor: "Ambition is pernicious in a republic. But in a monarchy it has some good effects; it gives life to the government" (III, 7, 25). Remarkably enough (and this is undoubtedly Montesquieu's political bias), the monarchical system succeeds in controlling ambitions and culminates in the public good, despite competition and conflicts between the subjects: "Honor sets all the parts of the body politic in motion, and by its very action connects them; thus each individual advances the public good, while he only thinks of promoting his own interest" (III, 7, 25).

Honor is the transcendental model that confers uniformity on monarchical society. Montesquieu calls it the "universal preceptor" (IV, 2, 29), a kind of school where the world learns to conform. Monarchical virtue is completely oriented toward the principle of distinction (preference for the self to others). The rule of monarchy is that of reciprocal adulation, resulting in the aesthetization of human actions: "Here the actions of men are judged,

not as virtuous, but as shining; not as just, but as great; not as reasonable, but as extraordinary"(IV, 2, 29). Politeness itself feeds on
rivalry but, at the same time, tempers it. The specularity sought
in politeness makes possible a reciprocal refraction of models:
politeness "arises from a desire of distinguishing ourselves. It is
pride that renders us polite" (IV, 2, 30). Politeness is the universal
reign of flattery. It is the effort of elegance lavished on one's person but, above all, the laudatory gesture toward the other. It makes
the court into a garden of Narcissi. In the form of honor, the simulacrum infiltrates the court. True values are measured by the
yardstick of artifice. Grand postures are false, grand gestures borrowed. They are in thrall to the worship of the self.

In *Mes pensées*, Montesquieu describes even more clearly the
paradoxical effect of the desire to please, which, despite its narcissistic negativity, demands a capacity for relations with others:
"The desire to please is what lends cohesion to society, and such
is the fortune of the human race that this pride, which should
dissolve society, instead fortifies it and renders it unshakeable."[11]
The ambivalence of honor, its inherent flaw, corresponds perfectly
to Hegel's idea of the ruse of morality: evil eventually contributes
to the production of good.[12]

The absolute model of honor is the prince. From him all re-
wards issue forth; to him falls the duty of granting distinction and
honor. The prince is in a sense the center, the sun around which
honor revolves; he is the universal guarantor, the general equivalent: "There is nothing so strongly inculcated in monarchies, by
the laws, by religion and honor, as submission to the prince's
will" (IV, 2, 31). Democratic virtue required obedience to others—
each individual's submission to every other individual. Here, the
prince is the mimetic regulator, the primary wielder of adulation.
The nobleman who models himself on the person of the monarch
will seek absolute distinction—that without peer—at the cost of
his life. He must be exemplary and seek the kind of superiority
that brings him the closest to the princely model: "There is nothing that honor more strongly recommends to the nobility than to
serve their prince in a military capacity. And, indeed, this is their
favorite profession, because its dangers, its success, and even its
miscarriages are the road to grandeur" (IV, 2, 32). This monarchical mimesis had already been depicted in *The Persian Letters:*

"The prince impresses the character of his mind on the court; the court, on the city; the city on the provinces. The sovereign's soul is a die that gives shape to all the others."[13] In *The Phenomenology of Spirit*, Hegel insists on the monarch's singularity, on the incommunicability of princely power. It is clear, however, that the idolatry, the flattery addressed to the king, is founded on a narcissistic form of reciprocity: the monarch, "this particular individual, thereby knows himself, *this* individual, to be the universal power, knows that the nobles not only are ready and prepared for the service of the state-power, but that they group themselves round the throne as an *ornamental setting*, and that they are continually *telling* him who sits thereon what he *is*."[14]

Montesquieu is quick to expose the fragility of the principle of monarchy and the seeds of its corruption. For him this corruption is founded on the paradox of the very notion of honor. Monarchy becomes corrupt when its principle is degraded, when there is a shift from metaphysical honor to honors, when the standard of distinction is once and for all at the mercy of the prince's whims: "It is still more corrupted when honor is set up in contradiction to honors, and when men are capable of being loaded at the very same time with infamy and with dignities" (VIII, 7, 114). Here Montesquieu is making a subtle distinction. The common competitive ideal toward which the noblemen of the kingdom tend (honor) disappears; the monarch dictates behavioral norms. The sovereign is the master judge of distinction and honors, which could be deemed signs without referents. Crisis ensues, monarchical order collapses under the weight of the arbitrary, and despotism has arrived.

We must return to the paradox of the monarchical structure, the fact that competition between individual interests does not harm it but, rather, leads to the general good.[15] This unconscious dimension, "invisible" in the sense of Adam Smith, leads to the stability of the government. Montesquieu describes honor as "the prejudice [hence blindness] of every person and rank" (III, 6, 24). In its very form, honor—as an "educated" passion[16]—contains mimetic desire: "The honor of monarchies is favored by the passions, and favors them in its turn" (IV, 5, 34). Durkheim clearly saw this, for in his innovative study of Montesquieu, he describes the emulative mechanism that constitutes monarchy, the paradox inherent in the monarchical apparatus: "There are varying degrees of rank, honor, and wealth; each individual has before his eyes persons with a standard of living superior to his own and grows *envious*. . . . This ambition that fosters rivalry among classes and individuals also leads them to perform their particular functions as well as possible. . . . Emulation results in a harmony between the different elements of society."[17] (In Latin, *aemulatio* means imitation; it is a mimetic paradox, for it presupposes a benevolent desire to equal the model while at the same time succumbing to rivalry and jealousy.) The rivalrous functioning of the monarchical order could not have been better expressed than by Durkheim. The separation of ranks stimulates envy and imitation. The superior group becomes the model for the subordinate group, and the imitative process is thus reproduced ad infinitum. Yet this dynamic, already introduced within Montesquieu's democratic structure, could be seen as partaking of its fragility or, rather, of its virtual impossibility. It now becomes easier to understand why Montesquieu wished to include a chapter on education, alongside the chapters on the nature and principle of governments. He uses a psychological analysis to complete the theoretical mimetic mechanism that he has set up. Thus the monarchical government, through education, becomes saturated with mimesis, with specularity. The world is a school of honor, the court is its battlefield, and politeness is its safeguard. But the common denominator remains the same—envy.

By isolating envy as typifying social passion, at least in a monarchy, Montesquieu joins the English liberal political tradition of David Hume and Adam Smith. Jean-Pierre Dupuy, starting from Thorstein Veblen, uncovers a conceptual structure of envy that corresponds precisely to Montesquieu's perspective on monarchy: "[Envy] is a goad that incites you to take action and to surpass yourself."[18] When Althusser, blinded by his Marxism, tries to strip honor of its rivalry, the prestige of the warrior, he misses the complexity of Montesquieu's theses. Althusser deliberately defuses honor, which he sees simply as a class passion, a virtue antecedent to the members of a particular class. He holds on to competition only as a distant memory from the past: now it is no more than simple vanity. It is wrong, however, to separate the struggle for prestige from the domain of honor, and to suppress the passion for recognition inherent in the latter: for honor means seeing that there are always men in front of (or behind) oneself.

Obscene Despotism

Even though despotism has its own nature, in Montesquieu it results from the corruption of the democratic and the monarchical states alike. The very excess of these two systems engenders this "monster." Their mimetic machinery also—and this is crucial to our study—provides the clearest explanation of the problem of despotism.

We have already seen that the danger of democracy was inscribed in its very principle, whereby equality drifts toward extreme equality. Montesquieu identified this as the surest path to despotism: "Democracy has . . . two excesses to avoid—the spirit of inequality, which leads to aristocracy or monarchy, and the spirit of extreme equality, which leads to despotic power" (VIII, 2, 110). How does he explain this evolution? How is this transformation effected? The answer is simple: through mimesis, that is to say, through the desire of each individual to occupy the other's place: "Each citizen would fain be upon a level with those whom he has chosen to command him" (VIII, 2, 109). The order that assured the stability of the regime collapses straightaway in the reciprocal struggle of subjects. Montesquieu presents very clearly this crisis that attacks the democratic institution and brings about the disintegration of relations of reciprocity:

> The people are desirous of exercising the functions of the magistrates, who cease to be revered. The deliberations of the senate are slighted; all respect is then laid aside for the senators, and consequently for old age. If there is no more respect for old age, there will be none presently for parents; deference to husbands will be likewise thrown off, and submission to masters. This license will soon become general, and the trouble of command be as fatiguing as that of obedience. Wives, children, slaves will shake off all subjection. No longer will there be any such thing as manners, order, or virtue. (VIII, 2, 109)

Montesquieu seems horrified by this monstrous leveling, this scrambling of orders. The democratic crisis occurs in the effacement of social positions and roles, in the loss of existing hierarchies. The maelstrom of mimetic relations described here affects

the entire social landscape, invading both public and private do-
mains. All roles become reversible in this undifferentiated tableau
of human relations. Later, Montesquieu offers an even clearer
mimetic origin for despotism, by showing the violent competition that takes over groups desirous of the same power: "The
greater the advantages they seem to derive from their liberty, the
nearer they approach towards the critical moment of losing it.
Petty tyrants arise who have all the vices of a single tyrant. The
small remains of liberty soon become insupportable; a single
tyrant starts up, and the people are stripped of every thing, even of
the profits of their corruption" (VIII, 2, 110). Once again, the
weakness of the democratic regime is seen to stem from its own
success. The pursuit of self-interest and personal freedom leads
one to ignore the other as a person. Violent reciprocity looms on
the horizon, and "all against all" quickly becomes "one against
all." The cycle of violence closes upon itself. The desire of one
individual has triumphed over that of the others. But it is the
same desire: the others all recognize themselves in this same desire, and they submit to the law of one individual. Montesquieu
clearly shows the passage between everyone's desire to appropri-
ate absolute authority and the final seizure of power by a single
person. He makes allowances, however, for a transitional phase:
the shift from democracy to despotism would seem to take place
at the conclusion of a struggle to the death among "petty tyrants";
later, one of those vying for mastery succeeds in making the others into his obedient subjects.

It would be useful at this stage to examine the concept of fear—
the principle of despotic government. The function of fear is to
homogenize, to undifferentiate the subjects before the tyrant's
terrifying gaze. The will of the tyrant is to abolish completely the
principle of individuality, the will to distinction. Despotism is
the absolute reign of one against all. In this it is precisely opposed
to monarchy and to the hierarchical structure that constitutes
monarchy. The despotic demand for homogenization also means—
and this is of capital importance—the retreat of ambition, the
impulse behind competitive reciprocity in monarchy: "Persons
capable of setting a value upon themselves would be likely to create disturbances. Fear must therefore depress their spirits, and

extinguish even the least sense of ambition" (III, 9, 26). Despotism requires that everyone be reduced to servility before the law; all subjects must be massed together under the same commanding power. They recognize their equality in their obedience to their prince. Fear is what is most easily propagated in such a society. It establishes a type of reciprocity that is constantly reversible: the despot is as afraid of all the others as they are of him. Fearful specularity binds everyone together in a sort of *danse macabre.*

The despot sees himself as the absolute model. He imposes his desire on everyone, or rather, he usurps the desires of others: herein lies his monstrosity. The despot, says Montesquieu, believes he is *everything;* he annihilates others by taking the place of all of them. He is a "man whom his senses continually inform that he himself is everything and that his subjects are nothing" (II, 5, 18). There is something dizzying in the contagion of despotic power, the delirious multiplication of the prince's will. To take over the despot's position of power, as the vizir does, means simply to learn to desire like him, that is, instantaneously. When the vizir decides, he expresses no particular will; all he does at that instant is to desire in the place of the sultan, just as the despot himself would have desired had he had the opportunity to decide at that precise moment. In other words, the delegation of the despot's power is strictly mimetic: "Again, as the law is only the prince's will, and as the prince can only will what he knows, the consequence is, that there are an infinite number of people who must will for him, and make their wills keep pace with his. In fine, as the law is the momentary will of the prince, it is necessary that those who will for him should follow his sudden manner of willing" (V, 16, 65). At any rate, the prince takes everything: "Of all despotic governments there is none that labors more under its own weight than that wherein the prince declares himself proprietor of all the lands, and heir to all his subjects. Hence the neglect of agriculture arises; and if the prince intermeddles likewise in trade, all manner of industry is ruined" (V, 14, 59). In their *Anti-Oedipus,* Gilles Deleuze and Félix Guattari develop an energetic definition of the despot that accords perfectly with Montesquieu's description. For them, the despot is situated at a confluence of streams, of which he is at once source and estuary. Everything tends to satisfy the sovereign's desire for consumption: "He is the sole quasi cause, the source and fountainhead and estuary of the apparent objective movement . . . all the flows converge into a great river that constitutes the sovereign's consumption."[19]

Despotism is the only violent regime discussed by Montesquieu. In order to ensure its fragile stability, the prince must shed blood. The internal economy of despotism is built on violence: blood flows in a sacrificial cycle that can never end. Those in the greatest danger are those who risk wanting to equal the prince: "It is necessary that the people should be judged by laws, and the great men by the caprice of the prince, that the lives of the lowest subject should be safe, and the pasha's head ever in danger" (III, 9, 27). Despotism is the reign of force, punishment, and vengeance. In fact, this last must be virtually permanent. The despotic state is subject to frequent revolts, and civil war is a constant threat: "A prince of this stamp, unaccustomed to resistance in his palace, is enraged to see his will opposed by armed force; hence he is generally governed by wrath or vengeance. . . . War, therefore, is carried on under such a government in its full natural fury" (V, 14, 57–58). The cycle of violence that propels the despotic regime is maintained by rivalries perpetuated by the prince. These rivalries seem to figure in all aspects of the state and encompass both the public and the private spheres (the prince's rivalry vis-à-vis his brothers as well as the notables of the realm). The judicial form of the despotic state is the *lex talionis*, the law of vengeance par excellence, expressing the purely violent reciprocity of relations, the immediate presence of force: "The use of the law of retaliation is very frequent in despotic countries, where they are fond of simple laws. Moderate governments admit of it sometimes; but with this difference, that the former exercise it in full rigor, whereas among the latter it ever receives some kind of limitation" (VI, 19, 92).

This form of government is also, paradoxically, the simplest. It corresponds to the most common figure of desire: submission before the all-powerful other. Montesquieu believes that moderate governments are rare. They appeal to the pluralization of powers, to a competitive distribution of forces, to a complex equilibrium of laws. These are not the elements of despotism:

. . . notwithstanding the love of liberty, so natural to mankind, notwithstanding their innate detestation of force and violence, most nations are subject to this very government. This is easily accounted for. To form a moderate government, it is necessary to combine the several powers; to regulate, temper, and set them in motion; to give, as it were, ballast to one, in order to enable it to counterpoise the other. This is a masterpiece of legislation, rarely produced by hazard, and seldom attained by prudence. On the contrary, a despotic government offers itself, as it were, at first sight; it is uniform throughout; and as passions only are requisite to establish it, this is what every capacity may reach. (V, 14, 62)

The obscene passions of this government are the very visible mark of its politics. Despotism offers the monstrous spectacle of oppressive reciprocity, of a vengeful machine turned on itself, in the loss of its own energy. The only harmony despotism knows is in the form of general oppression, fear, and eventually death. In Montesquieu's *Considerations on the Causes of the Greatness of the Romans and Their Decline,* there is a fantastic description of the homogeneity created by despotism. The obliteration of vital divisions has the effect of a virtual massacre: "And, if we see any union there, it is not citizens who are united but dead bodies buried one next to the other."[20]

Divide and Rule

The much-touted separation of powers (state functions corresponding to separate organs) is likewise subject to mimetic logic. This doctrine—which Montesquieu was the first to theorize in France—is most obviously applied within a monarchical structure. As has been shown, there is in fact less of a separation of powers than an independence.[21] Taking another tack, we shall see the contaminating presence of envy. This contamination prompts Montesquieu to offer the following exception to the rule: nobles cannot be judged by the people, but only by their peers, as the great are always "obnoxious to popular envy" (XI, 6, 156). Offering the example of Rome, the author does not hesitate to recall the rivalry between the plebeians and the patricians. Intervening in their political interaction, once again, is envy, which seems to arise out of the proximity and interchangeability of those who take part in power relations: this, as we have seen, is the problem with democracy. On the other hand, the further removed the model of power is, the less temptation there is for rivalry. Such is the case with monarchy:

> Those who obey a king are less tormented by envy and jealousy than those who live under an hereditary aristocracy. The prince is so distant from his subjects that he is almost unseen by them. And he is so far above them that they can conceive of no relationship on his part capable of shocking them. But the nobles who govern are visible to all, and are not so elevated that odious comparisons are not constantly made. Therefore it has at all times been seen, and is still seen, that the people detest senators. Those republics where birth confers no part in the government are in this respect the most fortunate, for the people are less likely to envy an authority they give to whomever they wish and take back whenever they fancy.[22]

Rome thrived on such conflicts between groups: "Thus the people disputed every branch of the legislative power with the senate, because they were jealous of their liberty; but they had no disputes about the executive, because they were animated with the love of glory" (XI, 17, 173). Montesquieu may have derived this idea from Niccolò Machiavelli, who argued that disagreements between the Roman senate and the people promoted freedom in the city. Moreover, it is in the English mode of government, which inspired Montesquieu's thesis on the separation of powers, that the philosopher seized on the importance of the division between the House of Lords and the House of Commons, which reminded him of the conflicts between patricians and plebeians in Rome.[23] Raymond Aron illuminates Montesquieu's thinking: "What in fact interested him is the rivalry, the competition, between the social classes which is a condition of a moderate government precisely because the different classes are able to balance each other."[24] In the separation of powers, we find the same ambivalence that constitutes honor in the monarchy. In a passage from *Considerations*, Montesquieu describes the paradox of the balance of powers in a state. This time, Gottfried Wilhelm Leibniz provides the analogy:

> What is called union in a body politic is a very equivocal thing. The true kind is a union of harmony, whereby all the parts, however opposed they may appear, cooperate for the general good of society—as dissonances in music cooperate in producing overall concord. . . . It is as with the parts of the universe, eternally linked together by the action of some and the reaction of others.[25]

Clearly, the symphony can turn to cacophony, to violent fury. The separation of powers is threatened by contamination with passions and interests, by the desire for reprisals.

Nevertheless, the English political system seems to guarantee a strange sort of equilibrium: "All the passions being unrestrained, hatred, envy, jealousy, and an ambitious desire of riches and honors, appear in their extent; were it otherwise, the state would be in the condition of a man weakened by sickness, who is without passions because he is without strength" (XIX, 27, 308). This is what Bernard Manin calls Montesquieu's choice of "antagonistic plurality."[26] In Montesquieu's eyes, the formation of opposing factions is not an evil but, on the contrary, proof of extraordinary political creativity, expressing the complex vagaries involved in the sharing of sovereignty. Montesquieu expresses the play of the separation of powers in the mechanistic terms of his time. His metaphors need only be psychologized in order to reveal an expression of rivalries and competition: "To form a moderate government, it is necessary to combine the several powers; to regulate, temper, and set them in motion; to give, as it were, ballast to one, in order to enable it to counterpoise the other" (V, 14, 62). This general restlessness, in the Leibnizian sense, is necessary so that sovereignty will not appear uniform, so that silence will not become the sole voice of the state. England in any case does not aim for political rationality; it has chosen the risk of passions, the free play of selfish interests and passions. This is the price of its liberty: "A people like this, being always in a ferment, are more easily conducted by their passions than by reason, which never produces any great effect in the mind of man; it is therefore easy for those who govern to make them undertake enterprises contrary to their true interest" (XIX, 27, 309).

Despotism and Nostalgia (*The Persian Letters*)

Will the enigma of *The Persian Letters* ever be solved? The text that ushers in the Enlightenment is perhaps also—already—its last will and testament. The baron seems to have cloaked his political novel in undecipherable secrecy. Therein lies the power of his text and the affirmation of its modernity. But perhaps we are misreading *The Persian Letters*. Critics have always tended to read the novel from the point of view of Usbek and to see Rica, his fellow traveler, as a sort of ebullient marionette: he is caught up in the whirlwind of society, astounded by the new signs shimmering before his unaccustomed eyes. And yet, what if we were to take Rica seriously?

Montesquieu appears to be offering us a lesson in the force of illusion that is inherent in power. In the novel, despotism plays this role, and the author is bent on making it clear at every turn. Usbek, ruler of Ispahan, may start out brandishing his phallic scepter to the thunder of his all-powerful voice, but he is soon marked by all the signs of melancholy. He progressively loses his grasp on any means of command; this process reveals the illusion on which his triumphant reign was founded.

Usbek's psychological demeanor could be said to be characterized by retrospective action. By this I mean that he refashions his past experiences in the present, conferring on them a new psychological value. Events are marked by a time lag that endows them with a significant affective value. Thus Persia, which he has just left, becomes present to him only in his Western exile. He becomes increasingly attracted to the harem that he abandoned: "As Usbek gets farther and farther away from the harem, his thoughts turn more and more toward his sacred ladies" (letter XXII, 75). He grasps his own country only through the nostalgia gnawing at him. Having set out to become an expatriate, he already seems to give up on the will to discover the other. He continually turns inward toward himself and his culture: "Dear native land, upon which the sun casts his first glances, you are not soiled by those horrible crimes that oblige that heavenly body to hide his face as soon as he appears in the black West!" (XLVIII, 113).

In *The Persian Letters*, departure is not only a metaphor for knowledge, for receptiveness toward another form of knowing; it comes also to signify the very distance from power. The absent Usbek comes to exist as an imaginary power. His subjects must continually reinvent the sacred image of the despot-king, reinstituting the seduction that gives him command. This manifestation of the imaginary distance of power is magnificently displayed in the relation of the women to their exiled sultan, and in the eroticism that constitutes and fetishizes their desire for the absent body. Fatma writes to Usbek: "I never go to bed without being perfumed with the most delicious scents. I remember those happy times when you would come to my arms. A happy dream, seducing me, brings before me the dear object of my love. My imagination is lost in his desires, it takes hope from his hopes" (VII, 52–53). Not merely adorning herself, this woman is already embalming the phantasmic body of a dead king. Josué Harari has pointed out the imaginary, idolatrous construction of the wives' relation to the despot: "Usbek's body is incarnated in a borrowed (imaginary) body, the empty body of an idol-mummy."[27]

Usbek on the Couch

Rica is in fact the best analyst of Usbek in *The Persian Letters*. His worldly discourse seems preoccupied with the turbulence of Western life, but underneath it all he is describing the harem in inverted form, often exposing its political fragility or even its injustice. He is the master of simulacra, but these are to be found less in the Europe that he adulates than in the Asia that he left behind and on which he unconsciously imposes the major effects of simulation.

The worldly, narcissistic society that Rica describes and decries operates like the harem. Worldly idolatry, however, in a sense pluralizes and democratizes what appears in Asian society as the privilege of one individual. He writes: "On all sides I meet people who talk ceaselessly about themselves. Their conversation is a mirror that always reflects their impertinent countenance. . . . They are a universal model, an inexhaustible subject of comparison, a spring of examples which never dries up" (L, 114–15). The idolatry directed at Usbek functions according to a model of one-all. Usbek becomes the idol and the ideal of the community, a status reinforced by his absence: "We miss you," writes Mirza to Usbek; "you were the soul of our circle" (X, 58). This seduction by power has been marvelously analyzed by Grosrichard, who sees this "morbid love" as active in all political power, with despotism as its purest expression.

The women's love for Usbek is an eroticized form of the flattery aimed at the monarch's transcendence. Montesquieu makes brilliant use of the Asiatic allegory of the harem in conceptualizing the hyperbolic relation between the One and the Many, between a prince and his subjects. *The Persian Letters* could even be described as saturated with this relation. The wives must band together to transmit to their sultan the image of his power, the confirmation of his sovereignty. They must be able—by annihilating their multiplicity—to affirm the prince as Unique, submitting themselves to his desire alone. The undifferentiated character of the women has been correctly observed in the resemblance of their names: Zachi, Zephis, Zelis.[28] Desire is renounced and delegated to the person of one individual. Zachi expresses the substitutive process of Usbek's women:

> We all appeared before you after having exhausted our imaginations in finery and ornament. . . . But you soon made those borrowed charms give way before more natural graces: you destroyed all our handiwork. We had to strip ourselves of that finery which had become an annoyance to you. . . . We saw you wander long from one delight to the next; your wavering soul remained for a long time in a state of indecision; each new grace extorted its tribute from you; we were all, in the twinkling of an eye, covered with your kisses. (III, 49)

Grosrichard remarks that "it is the members of the harem themselves who create the despot's transcendence, instituting and maintaining his radical otherness."[29] In Grosrichard's view, weaknesses and negativity that inhabit the residents of the harem establish the despot as an incomparable, other, absolute, unique being. Usbek himself continually seems to raise the problem of divinity, of God's relation to his creatures. What he is really questioning each time is his own destiny, his own transcendent idealization (LXIX, 148–51).

The frailty of Usbek's power stems from its very essence, and what most cruelly exposes this fragility is the relation of the Unique to the eunuchs. The void, which Usbek accuses the eunuchs of having in order to express their sexual negation, ends up contaminating his own power over his harem. His encapsulation of the way in which the eunuchs command (through obedience to the despot and delegation of command) is most interesting: "By an exchange of authority, you command as master like myself whenever you fear a weakening of the laws of decency and modesty" (II, 48). This ricocheting deferral of the exercise of power forms the very tempo of despotic command.

It is necessary to consider more fully the eunuchs, who are somehow obscene in their very exhibition of the lack that inhabits them, in their anomaly. The monstrosity of the eunuch derives from his troubling difference: neither man nor woman, he resembles nobody, and his anchor in reality is a separation. The eunuch is a being divided between his power and his duty to obey, between his desires and his inability to consummate them, between his imagination and his body. He must keep watch over what he can never possess. In his very body he somehow mimics female obedience and the master's authority. Unable to consummate his desire, he is condemned to dwell in the harem as a spectator of others' pleasures. Montesquieu's text continually emphasizes the negation of these monstrous beings, their absolute impotence (their nonsexuality is labeled nothingness, frigidity, stillness). The eunuch embodies a sort of nostalgia for sex. He is condemned to the memory of what he once had. He can experience pleasure only by summoning up the past. One of Usbek's eunuchs bemoans this invidious enactment of pleasure: "I entered into the harem, where everything aroused the regret of what I had lost" (IX, 55). Zelis speaks of the wretch "who will always remember what he was and thus make himself remember what he is no longer" (LIII, 119). *The Persian Letters* alludes to a "third sense" that supposedly affords the eunuchs a new order of pleasures, as if indemnifying them; but their loss seems irreparable and dooms them to remain eternally frustrated. The eunuch's authority, his pleasure in commanding, seems to be his only means of transferring his sexual energy and forgetting his physioerotic incapacity. The eunuch "changes pleasures," displacing his erotic power into the pleasure of commanding women: "I remember always that I was born to command them, and it seems to me that I become a man again when I can still do so. . . . In the seraglio it is as if I were in a small empire, and my ambition, the sole passion left to me, is satisfied a little" (IX, 56).

Further on in the text, the crisis in the harem will be expressed most forcefully through the eunuchs, in the ambivalence of their bodies. This crisis will first become manifest in the confusion of hierarchies, the increasing reversibility of the functions of command and obedience. The eunuchs are the most insistent reminder of this ambivalence. In the critical undifferentiation that strikes the harem, their monstrosity will become most painfully obvious. Already marked as victims and marginalized for confusing the natural order, they will become the perfect target for the riots that eventually overturn the very place whose peaceful serenity they formerly helped maintain.

In the figure of the eunuch, Montesquieu seems to freeze the energy of power into a sort of original lack. From the beginning, the *libido dominandi* is fueled by a weakness, as energy is displaced from one scene to another. The eunuch also illustrates the complicated dialectic of power: he commands, but his command establishes a certain dependence in relation to the other, a dialectic that constitutes power itself. This is how the head eunuch describes his relation to the women he guards: "There exists between us something like an ebb and flow of dominion and submission. . . . I am forever weighed down under orders, commands, chores, and fancies. They seem to spell each other at harassing me; they seem to arrange their whims" (IX, 57).

Doubles

It would seem that Montesquieu took pleasure in doubling the characters in *The Persian Letters*. The eunuchs are thus doubles of the despot; through these representatives, Usbek is multiplied ad infinitum. There is another character who doubles Usbek, in a rather more curious fashion: this is his traveling companion, Rica. Although they set off with a common purpose, the two men become alienated from each other during the journey. Ispahan recedes ever further from Rica as he substitutes the European reality for his native land. Could this be seen as one of Montesquieu's harshest criticisms of Asiatic despotism? Rica himself acknowledges his metamorphosis: "My mind is slowly losing everything Asiatic that was left in it, and I am adapting painlessly to European customs" (LXIII, 133). Unlike Usbek, Rica eventually decides to "put off the Persian costume" (XXX, 88). Rica's letters are never imbued with the nostalgia that fills Usbek's. The worldly society that Rica seems to criticize as a counterexample to Persia also conveys a full-fledged criticism of despotic Persian society.

Rica's rejection of the despotic system seems to be crystallized around the subject of women in particular. Objecting to the arbitrary relations between man and woman, Rica relativizes the relations between the sexes; he insists on breaking down the existing hierarchy by affirming that "our women belong too strictly to us, that such calm possession leaves us nothing to desire or fear, and that a bit of coquetry is the salt that adds savor and prevents corruption" (XXXVIII, 97). Rica even takes pleasure in setting the phalloerotic regime of one (master) versus all (women) over against the European sexual regime, based on the libertine circulation of bodies—a type of exchange in which property seems temporarily suspended: "A husband who insisted upon keeping his wife to himself would be looked upon as a disturber of the public pleasure, as a madman who would profit by the light of the sun to the exclusion of other men" (LV, 123). Now it is clear that the jealous husband of *The Persian Letters* is none other than Usbek himself: Rica's words would seem to be addressed to his companion. The Parisian gallantry so joyfully described by Rica is contrasted with Usbek's quiet harem; from the sultan himself comes a cold description of the seraglio, in sharp contrast to the worldly warmth of Paris. The harem chafes under his passion for authority: "One must admit that the seraglio is made more for hygiene than for pleasure. It is a uniform existence, without excitement. Everything smells of obedience and duty. Even the pleasures taken there are sober, and the joys severe, and they are practically never relished except as manifestations of authority and subservience" (XXXIV, 91).

Once again, however, Usbek's lucidity in no way pressures him to modify his relation to his women; he maintains the status quo. Far from changing it, he decides to reinforce what constitutes an obstacle to pleasure and *jouissance:* authority and dependence. He persists in giving orders; he wants to discipline the harem to the point of saturating it with the sound of his voice; he wants his ghost to command the slightest gesture. Suzanne Gearhart has pointed to this in her reading of the novel:

> Usbek's rejection of Rica's Paris causes him to cling to the despotic values of which his own voyage was to be the negation, for that rejection, as well as his estrangement from his fellow Persian Rica, constitutes an inverted recognition that the values he represents are threatened not only in France, but also where he is most vulnerable, in his seraglio in Ispahan. . . . The Parisian code is obviously unacceptable to Usbek, whose relation to his wives is defined, as he himself admits, solely by jealousy.[30]

At the end of the book, through a fable he gives Usbek to read, Rica proposes a transformation, a "transvestism" of the harem.[31]

He offers a regime based on pleasure, instead of a regime domi-
nated by fear. Rica's tale proposes a "new harmony," not only between chief and subjects, but also between the sexes. The story is
even directly targeted at Usbek's unhealthy jealousy, at the despot's
selfish desire to possess. It is worth quoting in its entirety:

> . . . a man named Ibrahim was jealous to the point of being impossi-
> ble. He had twelve extremely beautiful women, whom he treated
> very harshly. No longer trusting either eunuchs or walls, he kept
> them almost always under lock and key in their own rooms, where
> they could neither see nor talk to one another, for he was even jeal-
> ous of innocent friendship. All his actions took on the coloring of
> his natural brutality; never did a gentle word leave his mouth, and
> never did he make the slightest gesture without adding something
> more to the rigors of their slavery.
>
> One day, when he had called them all together in a room of his
> seraglio, one of them, more daring than the others, reproached him
> for his bad character. . . .
>
> This speech, which should have touched him, made him burst
> into furious anger. He drew his dagger, and plunged it into her
> breast. "My dear companions," she said in a dying voice, "if heaven
> takes pity on my virtue, you will be avenged." With these words,
> she left this unhappy life to enter into the sojourn of delight,
> where . . . she came upon a superb palace, prepared for her and filled
> with celestial men destined to her pleasures. . . . She allowed herself
> to proceed to very sweet reflections on her past lot and her present
> felicity. She could not keep from sympathizing with the unhappi-
> ness of her erstwhile companions. . . . she felt drawn to come to
> their help.
>
> She gave the order to one of the young men near her to take on the
> likeness of her husband, to go into the seraglio, to make himself
> master there, to expel the other man, and to remain in his place
> until she recalled him.
>
> The execution of her order was prompt. He clove the atmosphere,
> came to the door of Ibrahim's harem while Ibrahim was not there.
> He knocks; all doors are opened to him; the eunuchs fall at his feet.
> He flies to the apartments where Ibrahim's wives were locked up.
> While passing by, he had taken the keys out of the pockets of the
> jealous man, to whom he was invisible. He enters and surprises the
> women, at first by his gentle and affable manner, and soon there-
> after, surprises them even more by his eagerness and the rapidity of
> his enterprises. All the women partook of this astonishment; they
> would have taken him for a dream if he had manifested less reality.
>
> While these novel scenes were being played in the harem, Ibrahim
> knocks, announces himself, storms and shouts. After much diffi-

culty, he enters and throws the eunuchs into complete disorder. He strides through the house, but he retreats, and so to speak, falls from the clouds when he sees the false Ibrahim, his own true image, ensconced in all the liberties of the master. He cries for help; he wants the eunuchs to help him kill the impostor, but he is not obeyed. He has only one very weak resource—that is to fall back on the verdict of his wives. In one hour, the false Ibrahim had seduced all his judges. The other Ibrahim is pushed and dragged out of the seraglio and would have died a thousand deaths if his rival had not ordered that his life be saved. Finally, the new Ibrahim, master of the field of battle, proved himself more and more worthy of such a choice and distinguished himself by miracles heretofore unknown. . . .

The new master adopted a behavior so different from that of the first that it surprised all his neighbors. He got rid of all his eunuchs, opened his house to everyone; he didn't even want to let his wives wear the veil. It was a rather strange sight to see them with men at banquets, just as free as the men themselves. Ibrahim rightfully believed that the customs of the country were not made for citizens like himself. Meanwhile, he refused no expense; with immense prodigality he ran through the wealth of the jealous man, who, returning three years later from the far-off lands where he had been transported, found nothing but his wives and thirty-six children. (CXLI, 250–56)

This digression anticipates the ending of *The Persian Letters* and the revolt in Usbek's harem, led by Roxane. Disorder reigns in Ispahan. The laws of the seraglio are abolished, undifferentiation rules, and the hierarchies that kept the despot's empire intact collapse: "Things have come to a pass that is no longer tolerable," writes the head eunuch. "I found Zachi in bed with one of her women slaves—a thing so strongly prohibited by the laws of the seraglio" (CXLVII, 270). Solim later writes his master: "A new sense of joyfulness, spread throughout these halls, is, to my mind, infallible proof of some new satisfaction. In the most minute things, I notice liberties unknown up to now. Even among your slaves there reigns a certain indolence toward duty and observation of rules which surprises me (CLI, 272). The crisis sweeps through the harem with surprising speed. The text reproduces the escalation of violence through the rapid-fire exchange of letters bearing witness to it.

Usbek's absence makes it possible for this revolution to occur in the harem. He was once the principle of equivalence, establishing hierarchies; his exile now leads to a return of rivalries. He is told in a letter from the chief black eunuch: "The harem is in frightful confusion and disorder. War rules among your wives. . . . Not one of your wives fails to consider herself above the others by her birth, her beauty, her wealth. . . . And there is not one who does not try to use some of these claims in order to have all the marks of honor for herself" (LXIVV, 134–35). Once an idol, Usbek is now an object of sacrilege, the focus of negative desires. All the violence of the harem will be visited on his (absent) person. All of this renewed originary energy is catalyzed by this symbolic "death" of the sultan. Usbek is voided, one might say, at the end of Montesquieu's text, in a regular ritual of expulsion. The women's voices are raised in concert against a fallen, degraded king. Roxane, Zachi, and Zelis come one after another to declare their hate and to signal their separation. When Usbek mentions a possible return to Ispahan, he is forced to consider the possibility of his victimization: "I shall be carrying my head back to my enemies" (CLV, 275). No longer shall Ispahan see the prince's raised arm at dawn.

It could even be said that the despot's body is on some level dismembered at the end of the novel. Usbek becomes a sort of *diasparagmos*, a symbolic body savaged, torn to pieces. His letters, which symbolize his power with the threatening echo of his voice, are intercepted. Henceforth his words, like the rest of his body, are cursed. Usbek's fall brings to mind the execution of kings in certain African communities, as analyzed by various anthropologists. In this vein, we might speak of the "extraterritoriality" to which Usbek is relegated—and which is doubly figured by his exile; but we can also say that danger and excess appear as the very essence of his function. The violent death to which he is condemned is both the reaction against and the fulfillment of his now insatiable demands. The desired death of the despot, as the outermost limit of his desires, should put an end to the very excess of his power.[32]

The victimization of Usbek takes an even more powerful form— that of self-sacrifice. In the end, Usbek internalizes everyone's hate. He himself has become the pitiful model of their loathing, just as earlier his deification grew out of a common idolatry. Usbek's gradual withdrawal at the end of the novel could be analyzed as a true sacrifice that puts an end to the crisis of undifferentiation in the seraglio and to the internal war that eats away at it. This sacrifice takes a rhetorical form (Usbek stops answering the letters that arrive from Ispahan); it takes place in his absence. Usbek ends up annihilating himself: "It seems to me that I am destroying myself" (CLV, 274). He punishes and degrades himself, imagining his body as detritus. In the end, he is devoid of desire—for himself or others—and consumed with jealousy; his imagination haunted by absent rivals, he is overtaken by a sort of paranoid delirium, then sinks into a dark depression. Tormented by the most negative images, Usbek ends up identifying with the eunuchs that he used to abhor. He is left with nothing but those models of sacrifice, punishment, abjection, and castration: "Contemptible outcasts of human nature, you vile slaves with hearts forever closed to all feelings of love, you would bewail your state no longer if you knew the unhappiness of my own" (CLV, 275–76). Usbek resorts to vengeance (CLIII, 274), to reciprocity of an exclusively violent nature: for each act of betrayal by his women he concocts a phantasmic new punishment.

But by this time it is too late; a new order of things has been definitively established in his harem, a new founding harmony—at the price, it would seem, of another "sacrifice" (CLXI, 279), Roxane's suicide. It is the former wife, Roxane, who takes over the community's desires. Taking the sultan's place in the harem in order to install a new order, she even uses the master's seduction to achieve new ends: "I seduced your eunuchs. I took advantage of your jealousy, and out of your horrible harem I managed to make a place of pleasure and delight" (CLXI, 279). So speaks the sultan's rival, who usurps Usbek's privilege of uniqueness in order to reestablish the law of the many, an order no longer ruled by submission to a sole desire but allowing all desires to be expressed: "How could you have thought that I was naive enough to imagine that I was put in the world only to adore your whims?" (CLXI, 279). The "poison" (CLXI, 280) that consumes Roxane in the end makes her a perfect *pharmakos*, the scapegoat on whom this new order rests.[33] And Montesquieu participates in Roxane's extraordinary expiation: "The pen falls from my hands. I feel even my hatred weaken" (CLXI, 280).

This violent ending will find its echo in Rousseau's *Discourse on the Origin and Foundations of Inequality among Men,* in which the expulsion of a tyrant corresponds to the end of a history—that of the corruption of the civil state. What results is not group harmony but infinite reprisals: "The uprising that ends in the strangulation or dethronement of a sultan is as lawful an act as those by which he disposed of the lives and goods of his subjects the day before. Force alone maintained him; force alone brings him down."[34] In one sense Rousseau also sacrifices the despot by making him into a resigned victim. Unable to complain about the violence that befalls him, he can only accept his imprudence or bad luck.

Custom and Fashion

Usbek's despotism would be the illustration of a bad form of mimesis. It is narcissistic by nature. He would have neither model nor rival, or rather, he seeks his models elsewhere, in the oriental heaven: he wants to approach divinity. The mediators of this conversion are the Muslim priests with whom he corresponds from Europe. He writes to the Imam Mohammed-Ali: "I am in the midst of a profane people. Allow me to purify myself with thee; suffer me to turn my face toward the sacred places where thou dwellest; . . . care for my soul; intoxicate it with the spirit of the prophets. Nourish me with the knowledge of Paradise" (XVI, 68). Usbek is searching for "that pure source of all intelligence" (XVIII, 69). If his attitude were considered from a psychological viewpoint, Usbek's idealism could be seen as a mimetic transference in relation to Rica—they start out with the same desire for knowledge, the same will to know—or even better, in relation to his own whim. From then on, he pursues an ever more limitless model of sovereignty, a desire that dooms him to remain eternally unfulfilled. He feeds on the pathos of the infinite. Usbek seeks "the point of contact between Abyss and Empyrean" (XVI, 68). Inebriated with power, he is led to the unattainable horizon of his culture, before the abyss of his memory. Mohammed-Ali writes: "You have not read at all in the books written in heaven. What has been revealed to you is but a small part of the divine library" (XVIII, 71). Perhaps what he seeks in the almost priestly withdrawal of religion is the supreme means of fearing and of making himself feared (*The Spirit of the Laws* defines religion in despotic states as a "fear added to fear" [V, 14, 59]).

Rica's metamorphosis also seems to be the effect of a mimetic transference. He abandons his devotion to Usbek for an expansive mimesis. Usbek has grounds for complaining that Rica "seems to have forgotten his country, or rather, he seems to have forgotten me, so callous has he grown to my displeasure" (CLV, 275). Imitative contagion leads Rica to pluralize his models. In order to speed up his social integration, Rica goes so far as to renounce the factual distinction that his exoticism confers on him: "Free of all foreign embellishment, I found that I was more soberly judged. I had every reason to complain of my tailor, who in one moment, made me lose the attentions of public esteem" (XXX, 88). In fact, Rica is making his entrance into a more competitive market, in which resemblance fuels rivalry.

The fervor with which Rica throws himself into fashion is an indication of his thirst for democracy. The frivolity of Usbek's companion must be read not simply as a critique of Parisian society but also as a negative version of Asian society, vampirized by a single person, the sultan. Fashion counters hierarchy, creating a universe of happy competition. Rica's view may well be supported by Montesquieu, who in *The Spirit of the Laws* examines fashion as the sign of a greater communication within a group: "Fashion is a subject of importance; by encouraging a trifling turn of mind, it continually increases the branches of commerce" (XIX, 8, 295).[35] To this must be added Montesquieu's observations on the ambivalence of vanity. Among the good that comes of it, he cites "industry, the arts, fashions, politeness, taste" (XIX, 9, 295). Montesquieu makes Rica into a virtual theoretician of fashion, a liberal sociologist before the letter. Usbek, on the other hand, faced with the turbulent, multifarious energy of the present, cries out for a return to the past. Seeking a return to traditional order, he advocates a social cohesiveness based on the dictates of custom. His long, nostalgic lament for his land in *The Persian Letters*, the wistful melancholic return to his country, attests to his regressive tendencies, his conviction that past and tradition alone must reign. In more contemporary terms, we might speak of Usbek's "sociocentrism." On the one hand, he calls for tolerance and preaches cultural relativity; yet on the other, he is unable to break out of his own culture. Persia is his sole point of reference, his only anchor, the sacred sun of his childhood.

2 / The Spirit of Manners (Voltaire)

Origins

Our civilizations arise out of the dark mists of time; history is patient, and it is something of a miracle that societies, once congregated, prove at all durable. Such is the lesson gleaned from Voltaire's *Essay on Manners* and from *The Philosophy of History*, which serves as an introduction to the famous *Essay*. The rhythms of societies are like those of the earth, doomed to the vicissitudes of climatic upheavals. Unearthing the ruins of our history means imagining vast deserts of shifting sands and shores abandoned by the seas. This past itself, the very antiquity of the earth, is somehow terrifying to Voltaire. Sociability, it bears repeating, is miraculous: "A concurrence of favorable circumstances for ages, are necessary to form a great society of men, united under the same laws. The like is necessary to form a language."[1] In the beginning, human groups were separate; large gatherings necessitated a series of advancements, the first of which was the acquisition of a common language. Voltaire tells us that through imitation human beings developed new abilities. Indeed, the imitative faculty itself underwent a difficult start following the evolutionary adventure of the species.

The ability to reason is the culmination of a belated and slow learning process, of progressive intercommunication. In Voltaire's fiction of origins, reason seems to be granted to all from the beginning, but its diffusion is the result of arbitrary circumstances. There were, he claims, some sort of "models," to whom we owe the imitative propagation of knowledge: "The most ingenious man, born with the most flexible organs, must have formed some articulations, which their children repeated"; "in the course of time societies somewhat polished were formed, in which a small number of men were at leisure to think."[2] The advent of metaphysics is recounted as a sort of collective panic, a trauma that spread from an individual to an entire group. Thus the idea of the soul, of the immateriality of being, must have been drawn from the interpretation of two or three dreams occurring within a group.

Religious experience followed the same lines of development, except that here it is the common experience of fear—terror in the face of evil—that unites people. Voltaire's god, appearing late in the formation of societies, assumes the features of the sacrificial victim. The deity arrives at the end of a recurring process whereby evil is collectively expelled. The need to interpret the misfortunes that are visited upon their community leads the people to resort to a belief in supernatural powers. Thus we see the appearance of the sacred in history:

> The inhabitants of a village, who are little better than savages, perceive the fruits which should nourish them perish: an inundation carries away some cabins: others are destroyed by thunder. Who has done them this mischief? It could not be one of their fellow citizens, for they have all equally suffered. It is therefore some secret power that has afflicted them, and must therefore be appeased. How is it to be effected? by using it as they do those whom they are desirous of pleasing; in making it some small presents. There is a serpent in the neighborhood; it is very likely the serpent: they offer him milk near the cavern, whither he retires; from that time he becomes sacred: he is invoked when they are at war with the neighboring village, who, on their side, have chosen another protector.
>
> Other little colonies find themselves in the same situation. But there being no object near them to excite their terror and adoration, they call in general the being whom they suspect has done them mischief, the master, the lord, the chief, the ruler.[3]

What people project onto their protective divinity is the violence of nature, or their own violence (in the case of war); in this superior being they are exalting their own power. Voltaire develops this idea in his *Philosophical Dictionary:* "We adore, we seek to appease, only that which we fear."⁴ Often, protective deities are also gods of war. Opposing groups represent their respective strengths to each other in the form of rival divinities: "Each village sensed its weakness and its need for a strong protector. . . . It could hardly believe that the neighboring village did not also have its own god."⁵ For Voltaire, this would explain ancient theocracies with their intimate connection between religion and power—in a word, the sacred. From their very origins, human beings needed to submit themselves to forces that were even more terrifying than themselves. The all-powerful gods descend to earth, becoming "incarnated to come and govern men."⁶ The god of civilized reason, of vengeance and reward, is not far off. He, too, will be the scapegoat of human violence, the keeper of power that human beings refuse to assume.

The *Essay on Manners* continually reiterates this contamination of the sacred as the source of the original violence of our institutions. Our disturbingly barbaric origins make people indifferent to the most brutal violence. The memory of ancient times is replete with horrifying recollections: "Imagine deserts where wolves, tigers and foxes slit the throats of scattered, timorous cattle: this is the portrait of Europe during many a century."⁷ Further on, Voltaire contemplates the age of Louis the Debonnaire: "The history of the great events of this world is scarcely anything but a detail of crimes. I do not find any age which the ambition of the laity and the clergy has not filled with horrors."⁸ The beginnings of history are punctuated with cruelty, vengeance, reprisals, and wars between neighboring groups. It is well known that Voltaire saw the Middle Ages in particular as weltering in such barbarity, but the periods that follow are equally saturated with violence: "This entire history is a mass of crimes, madness and wretchedness."⁹ As Georges Benrekassa remarks, Voltaire "limits himself . . . to the observation of blood and pain for precarious results in the art of organizing and commanding men. . . . We dilute his thought: he said the art of subjugating them. Our share of 'rationality' was won in the face of a fearsome disorder, and the rationality of the organizing force is often nourished by this very disorder."[10]

Let us return to these irrational origins, these archaic beginnings. In *The Philosophy of History* Voltaire undertook to retrace this path. Before becoming a historian, he wrote as an anthropologist and psychologist of societies. The vast panorama of races and religions that begins the colossal project of the *Essay on Manners* is a highly original effort to understand human progress; it is unfortunate that so little attention has been paid to this preface, for it provides a splendid elucidation of the philosopher's historiographic work.

The Philosophy of History is a sweeping study of phenomena of faith. Like dreams, beliefs spread through the power of uncontrolled rumor. Superstition, the fetishized object of Voltairian criticism (which led him to coin the famous slogan, *Ecrasez l'infâme!*), is seen as one of the powerful forms of the sacred: it is an expression of the same crisis of panic, the same collective terror that is found in the first religious feelings. The simultaneous repulsion and fascination that idolatry, the magic of primitive ages, inspired in Voltaire is tied directly to this aspect. In the beginning, people collectively fed on illusions—oracles and dreams. Through imagination all of these were converted into belief; certain dreams became truth through the magic force of persuasion. Every time Voltaire examines the error of primitive times, he is forced to recognize the powerful role that the "universal consent of all men" plays in these phantoms of thought.[11] For him the worst aspect is the way the ancient imagination manages to leave its traces: there are monuments still standing that bear witness to these past errors, to the memory of these groups marked by terror and hallucination.

Our origins belong to the illusionists: sorcerers, magicians, sacrificing priests. The role of reason in history is therefore to reestablish truth, to efface the era of lies. The *Philosophical Dictionary* is thus a vast undertaking aiming to lay bare all religious phenomena. In it Voltaire condemns simulations of divinity in all their forms. The religious experience is cast as a heap of simulacra, a hodgepodge of false posturings. It is more important, however, to note the reasons for Voltaire's critique. I have said that the philosopher's historical research was based on psychological presuppositions. What he finds repellent about religious mimeticism, in fact, are the effects of propagation by imagination, mass phenomena of contagion including hysteria, convulsions, and public demonstrations of madness. Belief is based on prejudices: by this Voltaire means loss of judgment, distraction due to the passions. Superstition founded on human enthusiasm is the most reprehensible type of fatal error.

Voltaire writes at length on the prophets, whose profession it is to persuade others as they exalt themselves. Prophecies are portrayed as products of mass hallucination: "The Jews possessed this faculty of exalting and exciting the soul to such a degree that they saw every future event as clearly as possible."[12] Magic also turns out to be a manifestation of this type of hallucinatory reciprocity: "Distempered imaginations had in a dream seen their friends dying or dead: the magicians made the departed friends appear."[13] History is thus peopled with false messiahs. They are all magicians of the word, their power stemming from an extraordinary ability to seduce; they are masters of the false promise. The title of Messiah is usurped by idolatrous, deified kings. Voltaire points to the biblical King of Tyr as an example: "[Marked by a likeness to God], full of wisdom and perfect in beauty."[14] But alongside these exceptional examples must be ranged the humbler ones—the fakirs and the priests. All are implicated in the fable of universal imposture.

Even the Quakers, notwithstanding the sympathetic regard in which Voltaire holds them, are implicated in religious simulation. When Voltaire recounts the beginnings of the sect, he cannot avoid recalling the original fanaticism and imitative contagion that led to its founding. Voltaire gives us this portrait of Patriarch Fox:

> [He] believed himself inspired. The consequence was that he thought he should speak in a different way from other men; he began to tremble, to contort his body and make wry faces, to hold his breath, and then to expel it violently. . . . This was the first gift he bestowed upon his disciples. With perfect sincerity, they made all the grimaces their Master did; they trembled as hard as they could in the moment of inspiration.[15]

The Chinese alone stand out as having origins that seem consubstantial with rationality. Their history is inhabited by reason.

From the outset they do without fables, fictions, and religious sentiment: "The Chinese do not refer to those savage times, when it was necessary for men to be cheated in order to be guided."[16] In periods closer to our own, such as the twelfth and thriteenth centuries, idolatry became the province of popes and priests, all those who usurp divinity. Voltaire calls them "those gods on earth, now murderers, now murdered."[17]

The Philosophy of History concludes with the subject of those sacred legislators who imitate the deity by speaking in the name of the universal. They are no better than charlatans who are able to express truths acknowledged by everyone, "engraven in every heart."[18] These impostors toy cunningly with collective beliefs and manipulate everyone's desires:

> If I had met with one of those great quacks in a public square, I should have called out to him, Stop, do not compromise thus with the Divinity; thou wouldst cheat me, if thou makest him come down to teach us what we all knew; thou wouldst doubtless turn him to some other use; thou wouldst avail thyself of my agreeing to eternal truths, be but ill-acquainted with the human heart, to suppose it preach thee to the people as a tyrant who blasphemeth.[19]

In the text of the *Essay on Manners*, Voltaire describes Mahomet thus: "He had a warm and nervous eloquence . . . an air of authority and insinuation. . . . It is likely that like all enthusiasts, violently persuaded of their own ideas, he came upon them with good faith, strengthened them with his reveries, and fooled himself while fooling others."[20] In each description of fanatical efficacy, the narcissism of falsehood and persuasive self-seduction can be detected. In the 1742 play that Voltaire devotes to the Muslim prophet, *Le Fanatisme ou Mahomet le prophète*, the author sketches a portrait of the fanatic. Mahomet becomes the paragon of imposture through the ages. He operates as a mass poisoner. How did he manage to do it? Voltaire shows us that he was able to hypnotize the other by idealizing his subjects' desire for domination: "My faith creates heroes."[21] This is the seductive element in Mahomet's message. The prophet's political persuasiveness stems from his ability to represent the group's power, its desire for conquest. Mahomet compels obedience; he strips his faithful of their own will. Hence Seid can say: "King, pontiff, and prophet, to whom I pledge my allegiance, master of nations, recognized by heaven, you hold complete sway over my being."[22] Voltaire uses the term *zeal* (*zèle*) to designate the power of illusion that the prophet is capable of exercising over the crowd. According to its etymology, the word, from the Greek *zelos*, indicates imitation, in particular of the divinity. Zeal is moreover communicable to the other; it attracts fanatical identification. It is thus operative both on the side of the prophet and on the side of the faithful. The sovereignty that accrues to Mahomet is illegitimate, as it is founded on fear and the intimidation of the masses: "The multitude, blind and weak, is born to serve great men, to admire, to believe."[23] Mahomet's sacred royalty is based on terror and feeds on the violence of the passions. It is thus, in its very essence, a usurpation. And being irrational, it is noncontractual.

Hegel has this play in mind in *The Phenomenology of Spirit* when he denounces political superstition, which in its synthesis of popular error and religious seduction is for him the most symbolic manifestation of despotic arbitrariness: "From the stupidity and confusion of the people brought about by the trickery of priestcraft, despotism, which despises both, draws for itself the advantage of undisturbed domination and the fulfilment of its desires and caprices, but is itself at the same time this same dullness of insight, the same superstition and error."[24]

This is what reason will be called upon to illuminate; these are the shadows that laws will henceforth chase away. As Benrekassa so aptly puts it, "Voltaire therefore believes it possible to displace the religious presence in such a decisive fashion as to eliminate its ancient relation with the sacred, linked, as far as power is concerned, to a perverted use of the message."[25] Philosophy cures men of imposture, of false revelation, of the fanaticism that blinds them. Voltaire concludes his *Essay on Manners:* "Amongst all nations history is disfigured by the fable until the moment when philosophy comes to enlighten men; and when philosophy finally arrives in the midst of these shadows, she finds spirits so blinded by centuries of errors that she can barely disabuse them; she finds ceremonies, events, monuments, established to affirm falsehoods."[26] Philosophy itself, however, takes the form of a countercontagion. Such are the curative powers of exercising reason: "There is no other remedy for this epidemic malady than the spirit of philosophy, which, spreading from person to person, at length civilizes and softens the manners of men."[27] Religion is a poison. The remedy for this furor, this madness, lies in the peace of the senses afforded by philosophy.

The ambivalent position of philosophy toward the sacred resides in this interweaving of poison and remedy. If we properly understand Voltaire's terms, philosophy itself must contaminate, attacking *a contrario* the virus of fanaticism. When Hegel refers to Voltaire as one of the most powerful adversaries of superstition, as the most eloquent representative of Enlightenment thinkers confronting the "realm of error,"[28] he takes up the same metaphors of epidemic, propagation, and infection. The Hegelian dialectic posits instead a reciprocal contamination between the Enlightenment spirit ("pure insight") and belief: the former "infiltrates the noble parts through and through and soon has taken complete possession of all the vitals and members of the unconscious idol."[29] Jean Hyppolite's commentary on this central chapter of the *Phenomenology* employs an astonishingly mimetic lexicon, expressing the dialectic in terms of rivalry: thus belief and insight can "oppose and confront each other in a fratricidal combat all the more violent in that they fundamentally express the same truth, the truth of spirit."[30] Hyppolite even envisions the transformation of one domain by the other, through an excess of resemblance. Only absolute spirit can deliver consciousness from the mediating moment that the Enlightenment represents, by recognizing the power of revelation and at the same time putting supreme abstraction in its place.

Hegel's formulation of the duplicity of the Enlightenment sheds light on Voltaire's religious dilemma. Reason, which Hegel touts as the standard of secular conversion, is itself steeped in the discourse of fanaticism. Voltaire lashes out all the more vituperatively against the charlatans of speech and the priests of persuasion because he is in awe of their power. Reason should indeed become a substitute for the sacred, but it must do so by assuming the same strength of conviction, the same imaginal weight, the same desire to achieve unanimity. Philosophy must counter erroneous enthusiasm with the enthusiasm of reason. The impact religion has on the imagination is what Voltaire envies, and it is also what seems to unsettle him about religion. Voltaire ushers the philosopher into the most sacred place of all—before the monuments of deception, into the midst of the fanatical rabble. Can the philosopher make others believed? As Voltaire questions in the *Essay:* "How, for example, could a philosopher have persuaded the rabble in the temple of Jupiter Stator that Jupiter had not descended from the heavens? . . . What philosopher would have been able to deny, in the temple of Castor and Pollux, that these twins had fought at the head of the armies?"[31] Philosophy and reason harbor an extraordinary nostalgia for impassioned speech. Progress in history moves toward a general degradation of the passions. What philosophy lacks above all is this remarkable power to gather people together, this collectivizing force. In this spirit Voltaire complains that "it is quite lamentable that philosophy is unable to accomplish for us what it could do for the ancients; it rallied men together, while for us only superstition has this privilege."[32] Rather, philosophy shares in a general wasting away of the religious spirit: "The world is saturated with controversies and with sects."[33] This observation does not stop Voltaire from regretting that philosophy has never enjoyed the privilege of proselytism or the apostolic devotion of the early religions. Philosophy is doomed never to recover this desire for association: "Isn't it amusing . . . that the ignorant Mohammed should have given a religion to Asia and Africa; and that Messrs. Newton, Clarke, Locke, Le Clerc, *et al.*, the greatest philosophers and the best writers of their time, should just barely have managed to acquire a little flock of followers that, small as it is, dwindles each day?"[34] When Voltaire notes the power of magic, prophecies, and oracles in early times, he is forced to admit that truth, a latecomer, has not obtained "the universal consent of all men."[35] Deploring the absence of all philosophical emulation, of all collective imitation of truth, he writes again that "in historical times, the most noble truths have but few sectaries; the greatest men die without honor. The Themistocleses, the Cimons, the Miltiadeses, Aristideses, the Phocions, are persecuted; whilst Perseus, Bacchus, and other fanatical personages have temples."[36]

The other *philosophe* who is intent on condemning the contamination of the political by the religious is Diderot. He reproaches Montesquieu, for example, for beginning *The Spirit of the Laws* with a divine invocation. In his *Observations on the*

Nakaz, Diderot insists fervently on the separation between the altar and the throne. "Reason is the enemy of faith," he writes.[37] What the philosopher abhors is the religious blackmail that occurs when the group expresses its arbitrary will. Fanatics forget themselves as citizens and become terrorists of faith: "The troubles of society are never worse than when agitators can make use of the pretext of religion and mask their designs behind them."[38] Nevertheless, Diderot's condemnation, like Voltaire's, betrays the originary seduction of the religious impulse. The difference between faith and philosophy would seem to lie, rather, in the quality of their common fanaticism. In this dialectical confrontation, philosophy is the loser from the outset. It suffers from a lack of persuasiveness: the gap between philosophy and religion is the sacred itself. Philosophers "have neither confessionals nor public pulpits; that is because they neither seduce in secret nor preach to congregations. For at times they are very fanatical. It is true that their fanaticism does not have a sacred character. They speak not in the name of God, but in the name of Reason, which does not always speak coldly, but which is always listened to coldly."[39] Philosophy can still find a way out, by fetishizing reason. If it is unable to convince others, it can attempt to convince itself. It invents itself as its own icon, its own idol. All the philosopher need do, in his delirium of envy and unseemly mimicry, is don the priest's habit.

Voltaire's life seems to bear witness to this ultimate folly. The philosopher ends up identifying with the fanatics that he denounces. It is said that Voltaire would regularly come down with a fever every Saint Bartholomew's Day. And René Pomeau is right to describe Voltaire's antireligion as a veritable obsession, a true "passion."[40] He also relates a revealing episode that took place at Ferney. One Easter Sunday, Voltaire decided to take part in High Mass. Six huge candles preceded the patriarch, who delivered the sermon himself. One can imagine what the sacrilegious seduction of the event must have represented for Voltaire. For this brief, narcissistic instant, he experienced the passion of the priest. He wanted his speech to cure.

On the subject of fanaticism, Voltaire left this statement, which indicates that the mimetic power of the fanatics' fervent enthusiasm does not leave him cold: "There are times in which one must imitate their contortions and speak their language."[41] Or even better, he examines the fanatical countercurrent and the role played in it early on by the philosophers: "Those sages made use of superstition itself to correct its enormous abuses, in the same manner as the heart of a viper is applied to cure its bite; many fables were intermingled with useful truths, and these truths were supported by fable."[42] The contradiction did not escape Sade, who wrote of the imposture of religion:

> At its very birth, this shameful cult might have been utterly destroyed had one but employed against it those weapons of the contempt it deserved; but men took it into their heads to employ persecution; the cult throve; 'twas inevitable.
>
> Even today were one to cover it with ridicule, it would fall. The adroit Voltaire never used any other arm, and among all writers he is the one who may congratulate himself upon having the greatest number of proselytes.[43]

Voltaire's *Essay on Manners* and his *Philosophical Dictionary* continually reiterate the author's abhorrence for rites and ceremonies, which, uniting the community around original errors, perpetuate beliefs through repetition and consecrate their imaginative power. Voltaire wishes for manners to be tempered by reason. The forward march of history should bring a progressive moderation of the passions; primitive mobs should become less ferocious. But Voltaire himself exemplifies the weakness of this narrative. Reverting to the prehistory of groups, he ends up identifying with the very people he expected to leave behind in the mists of primitive time. Pretending to be a priest, Voltaire simulates a ceremony in the second degree.

Voltaire's philosophy of history is often compared to Hegel's. Both are teleologies in which reason progressively effaces the traces of falsehood; in the final analysis of history, the triumph of truths stacks up. I believe it fruitful to bring up another name as well—that of Friedrich Nietzsche, who articulates what remains unconscious in the French philosopher. The genealogy that Nietzsche proposes in his denunciation of the ascetic ideal from priest to philosopher also exposes the will to power that underlies Voltaire's position. We claimed that, for Voltaire, the problem with philosophy lay in its inability to efface the imposture of primitive times. (In the beginning was the Error!) The philosopher is unable to make use of the persuasive fear parlayed by founders of religion. In *On the Genealogy of Morals,* Nietzsche tells a similar tale. But Nietzschean degradation goes as far as to affect the history of philosophy itself:

> The earliest philosophers knew how to endow their existence and appearance with a meaning, a basis and background, through which others might come to *fear* them. . . .
> . . . to begin with, the philosophic spirit always had to use as a mask and cocoon the *previously established* types of the contemplative man—priest, sorcerer, soothsayer, and in any case a religious type—in order to be able to *exist at all.*[44]

When toward the end of *Ecce Homo* Nietzsche took up Voltaire's formula *Ecrasez l'infâme!* he was recalling and sympathizing with the earlier philosopher's anticlericalism, but he hardly imagined that this very anticlericalism harbored the enthusiastic desire that he himself sought in other respects to condemn.

Destiny and History (*Zadig* and *Candide*)

Voltaire's stories convey the essential ambivalence of his philosophy through a delightful transposition of these contradictions. They attest even more clearly to the inevitable return of the religious in Voltaire's rationality.

Zadig is portrayed as a perfectly constituted being (he is young, handsome, and wealthy) who is all the more perfect because his qualities keep him removed from worldly affectation. His wisdom protects him from facile vanity. The young philosopher's thinking is transparent; the soundness of his speech sets him apart from the crowd. He avoids inane conversation:

> In the reign of King Moabdar there lived in Babylon a young man named Zadig, of naturally charming disposition reinforced by education. Although young and rich, he knew how to control his passions, was unaffected, did not want always to be in the right, and was considerate to human frailty. People were astonished to observe that despite his good sense he never derided the loose, scrappy, noisy tittle-tattle, the reckless backbiting, the ignorant conclusions, the coarse quips, the empty tumult of words, which in Babylon were called "conversation."[45]

A quarrel among scholars forces Zadig to abandon philosophy. He seems to return to a certain amount of worldly intercourse but soon substitutes the demands of being for those of appearance, transparency for the mask, true speech for vain conversation:

> He brought together in his house the most honorable men and the most amiable women in Babylon. He gave dainty suppers preceded often by concerts, and enlivened by charming conversation whence he managed to banish the desire to show off one's own wit—which is the surest way both of having none and of spoiling the most brilliant society. Vanity influenced the choice of neither his friends nor his viands, for he preferred in everything to *be* rather than to *appear:* and in this way he won for himself the sincere esteem to which he did not pretend. (340)

Before long Zadig—against his own wishes, the narrator always seems to imply—becomes the community idol. In his new capacity as minister, after the trial to which the envious Arimaze subjects him, he is able to give his charm full scope and to show off all his wit. The others, however, will fall into the trap of appearances. The destiny of this minister-philosopher is caught up in the prevailing forgetfulness of being. Zadig is spokesman for truth, law, and reason, yet others are touched only by the appearance of his words: "He made everybody feel the sacred power of the law, and nobody the weight of his importance" (346). Do what he may, Zadig is soon idolized, imitated: "In this wise did Zadig show every day the subtlety of his genius and the goodness of his soul. In spite of being accounted a marvel, he was loved" (349). He becomes everyone's object of desire; he occupies the imagination of the community: "He passed for the luckiest of men. The whole empire swelled with his name. He was ogled by all the women and praised by all citizens for his fairness. The scholars looked on him as their oracle, and even the priests admitted he knew more than Yébor, the aged Archmagus. . . . they believed only what he thought credible" (349–50). Zadig wields a sort of hypnotic influence over the others by managing, miraculously, to captivate their desires. But Voltaire provides false reasons when he attributes natural goodness and wisdom to his hero. There is a streak of bad faith in Zadig: all his attempts to shine are also bids to attract the attention of others. Zadig's so-called goodness takes on the appearance of a false narcissism. His displays of reason pretend not to be aimed at any audience but, rather, to home in on the inner truth of the person. But the spectacle of the beautiful soul depends, as we shall see, on the presence of the other. It is, in fact, a specular projection of the other's desire.

What Zadig pulls off masterfully as a philosopher or sage is to offer himself to the other as an idealized image of the other's desire for knowledge. For Zadig, being a philosopher means showing the other that he, too, can know; it means putting himself in the other's place. Thus, as we have seen, "they believed only what he thought credible" (350). This belief in the image, this magic faith in knowledge, finds expression in the character's power of conviction: "Zadig was content to have the style of good sense. Everyone was on his side, not because he was what a man should be, not because he was wise, not because he was lovable, but just because he was grand vizier" (350). What is convincing is not so much the truth of reason as its effect through the other's desire. Knowledge itself comes to light superfluously. The relation to the other is channeled through desire; the desire for knowledge is only one of the forms through which desire can choose to actualize itself. Zadig shows us the specular nature of what could usefully be termed the philosophical *relation*. Reason itself takes the form of a mimetic tool or instrument. Whence the philosopher's coquettish air and his power of persuasion: "The charm of his conversation was heightened by that desire to please which is to the mind what jewels are to beauty" (353). Whence also the fact that Zadig's seduction works in all senses. If he is idolized as a fount of knowledge, if he injects the other miraculously with his learning, he is also immediately regarded as an object of desire by all the women of Babylon ("He was ogled by all the women" [349]). This double attraction works on Astarte.

Voltaire's story clearly exposes Zadig's techniques of rational persuasion. In order to satisfy the others' desire for learning, he need only make them believe that they are right. When he later resolves disputes in exile, what calls for our attention is not so much his sense of equity or habitual wisdom as this admirable strategy. A particularly telling example occurs at Sétoc's supper:

> Zadig, who had kept silence throughout the dispute, rose at last, and as the Celt seemed the maddest addressed him first. He said the Celt was quite right, and asked him for some mistletoe. He congratulated the Greek on his eloquence, and calmed all their heated spirits. To the man from Cathay he said very little, because that worthy had

been the most reasonable of them all. "My friends," he wound up, "you are going to quarrel about nothing, for you all hold the same views." (370)

Here the philosopher acts as mediator or conciliator. He adopts the position of the third party, personally becoming the locus of contradiction by offering the ideal posture of reason: thus he resolves all differences of opinion. Further, Zadig forces the others into conciliatory imitation, activating a mimetic crisis among the opponents. In Zadig's trials, all the disputes originate in the desire to imitate. The justice administered by the hero thus ends up producing difference, which paradoxically will place in opposition to each other the very partners who are carried away by their desire for the same. Such is the miracle of Zadig's person. He is indeed comparable to a magus or a sorcerer: his persuasive powers are magical. Zadig is what Michel Serres calls "the universal in communication": "His principal gift was that of deciphering the truth which all men try to obscure" (*Zadig*, 346).[46]

As far as Sétoc himself is concerned, the lesson in philosophy bears all the marks of a measured and manipulative seduction. Zadig initially tries to capture his master's curiosity, his desire to know. He zeroes in on the immediate sphere of what is useful to his listener, of what ought to appeal to his knowledge:

Zadig took the liberty . . . of teaching him the laws of equilibrium. The astonished merchant began to look at him from a different angle. Zadig, seeing the merchant's curiosity stirred, stimulated it by telling him many things not irrelevant to his business, such as the specific gravities of metals and commodities of equal bulk, the characteristics of various useful animals, the means of making useful such as were not: with the result that the merchant thought him a very learned man. (362–63)

If Zadig turns out to be an excellent teacher, it is because he makes perfect use of the other's mimetic talent. He manages to anticipate behaviors and to adapt his own accordingly. Another scene with Sétoc exposes all the ambivalence of the philosopher's behavior. In order to convert his master, he employs a superstitious analogy, a representation of the same. To force Sétoc to adore a unique god, Zadig makes a spectacle of his own profane adoration: Zadig's representation of himself will convert his master.

Idolatrous persuasion proves absolutely effective here, as Zadig's false image of himself produces a contrary belief:

> Zadig lit a large number of tapers in the tent where he was to sup with Sétoc, and as soon as his patron appeared threw himself on his knees before them and cried:
> "Eternal and Radiant Lights, grant me always your favors!"— after which he sat down to table without looking at Sétoc.
> "What are you doing?" asked Sétoc, astonished.
> "I do as you do," replied Zadig. "I worship these candles, and neglect their master and mine."
> Sétoc grasped the profound meaning of this apologue. (365)

The operation is a complete success. It is as if a transference of belief had taken place. This conversion is punctuated with mimetic gestures. Sétoc will acknowledge that "his slave's wisdom entered his soul" (365).

Zadig displays his impressive qualities to best advantage in the case of a widow who is about to sacrifice herself on a funeral pyre. The rational analysis that ridicules an old custom—the law requiring a widow to burn herself publicly atop her husband's corpse—comes after a preliminary procedure: first, it is the woman's coquetry that Zadig targets using flattery. His philosophical persuasion begins through a sexualization; indeed, the other's mind, rather than being penetrated by the power of reason, is summoned through an erotic appeal: "He had himself presented to her and, having gained admittance to her mind by praising her beauty and saying what a pity it was to set fire to so many charms, did homage further to her constancy and courage" (366). Zadig achieves a twofold result. The widow is convinced and rationally rejects the idea of burning on the funeral pyre. In addition her narcissism is aroused, and she responds to the philosopher's desire: "'What would you do,' he asked her, 'if the vanity of burning yourself ceased to possess you?' 'Lack-a-day!' answered the lady, 'I think I should ask you to marry me'" (367).

Zadig's Crown

The last episode in the tale illustrates even more clearly the text's mimetic configuration. Once again, the actantial sequence of the story must be reinterpreted. Winning the crown is described as a test of love, as Astarte is the final reward. This entire episode has a mythical cast: there are riddles to be solved and a tournament that the champion must win in order to obtain Astarte's hand and become king of Babylon. I believe it is possible to assign a meaning to this mythological interlude including the hero's asceticism. What should be read in this episode of "battles" is not so much a test of love as a ritual test that must be accorded its full anthropological weight. More important than obtaining his lady's hand is Zadig's reception by the people of Babylon: he must become the idol of the community once again, the star at the center of their desires. For these reasons, Zadig must pay with his own person, which he must submit to a sacrificial ritual. The hero does in fact defeat his rivals in the battles for the throne, but while the victor sleeps, Itobad rushes in to claim the title won by Zadig. Zadig arrives in the amphitheater, where he is jeered by the awaiting crowd, which treats him as a sort of clown: "All the people left in the gallery and the arena received him with hoots. He was surrounded and insulted to his face. Never did man endure such humiliating mortification. He lost patience, and with blows from his saber sent flying the rabble which dared abuse him. But he did not know what action to take" (401).

Zadig must first suffer the wounds of the hero-victim in order to be received as king of Babylon. He will soon be compensated for the humiliation of the previous scene. This time the crowd will cheer him and acknowledge him as their hero: "As soon as Zadig appeared in the town the people flocked round him. Their eyes could not see enough of him, their mouths bless him sufficiently, their hearts wish ardently enough that he might be their king. . . . The people carried him right to the assembly hall" (409). At last, it is "by consent of all" that he is proclaimed king (411). Once again idolized, once again placed at the center of the others' desire, Zadig can wish for no more. If the tale consistently portrays the hero's wanderings on a path toward the individual wisdom of the true philosopher, it must be said that Zadig always manages to take his position at the hub of radiating desires. Voltaire makes him a handsome young man; placed in the center of feminine desires, he becomes a phallic object. Because his natural wisdom provides an answer for everything, he fulfills everyone's desire for learning. Zadig finally becomes the idol of the community and, with his virtues, satisfies the political desire of the Babylonians.

It could also be said that by becoming king Zadig also fulfills his own wishes. This allows us, without recourse to the Providential-ist or Leibnizian argument, to account for the fact that he suffers so many misfortunes and that each success leads him into a new series of misadventures. The problem is his continual need to fill his emptiness as a desiring subject. Perhaps there is an element of masochism is Zadig. He considers himself to be "the model of misery" (385). He recites his hardships again and again in a veri-table litany; he keeps a running account of them. For Zadig, de-sire is destiny. The good that befalls him at the end of the story is not a divine reward for a series of evils strewn across his terres-trial path, the end of an incomprehensible trajectory for him; on the contrary, it is a happy, megalomaniacal piece of deft choreog-raphy, putting an end to a succession of unsatisfied desires.

It is important for us to attempt to decipher the destiny of Babylon. Zadig's exile plunges the town into a series of catastro-phes that culminate in the murder of Moabdar. Everything is set up for Zadig's triumphant return to restore order. In some sense he has to become estranged from his community in order to be readmitted into it. Moabdar's murder could itself be interpreted as wish fulfillment. Zadig is also the center around which the happiness of others takes shape. His light radiates over the rest of the community. Henceforth Sétoc, the fisherman, and Cador all enjoy a far brighter destiny. Thanks to Zadig, in any case, harmony is restored to the world. If his altruism in contrast to others' ego-tism is suspicious, it must nevertheless be admitted that as the perfect mediator he has succeeded in absorbing everyone else's troubles into his own destiny. It is not for nothing that, by the end of the tale, Zadig is basking in this idolatrous and narcissistic bliss: "Men gave their blessings to Zadig, while he gave his to heaven" (412).

At last he achieves the universality, the general equivalent of desires, that was sought from the beginning.[47] Zadig himself, as an idol, embodies this general equivalent. Fashioned in the image of time itself, he is a sort of transcendence incarnate, the impos-sible dream of eternity:

> Nothing is longer . . . since it is the measure of eternity, nothing is
> shorter since all our schemes lack it; nothing is slower to him who

waits, and nothing passes more quickly for him who is happy; on the one hand it extends right up to infinity, and on the other it may be divided and subdivided right down to infinity; all men disregard it, and all men regret losing it; nothing can be done without it; it condemns to oblivion all that is unworthy of posterity, and makes the great things immortal. (409–10)

When Zadig undergoes the test of the riddles at the end, he reconciles Babylonian society to its own beliefs. A miraculous passage to reason has taken place, along with a convergence of various types of knowledge. This is the last stage in the seduction of ancient principles. Zadig's words contain echoes of the community's ancient truths. In previous times, as we remember, he spoke like Yébor or Zoroaster. The philosopher's triumph consists not in having found the conviction of truth but in seeking the blandishments of universality, the contagious effect of persuasion. He has become a sort of fakir of reason.

On Royalty

Zadig's series of misfortunes are brought to a close by his accession to royal glory. His ultimate test is the contest to obtain the crown. The sacrificial structure of this struggle calls for analysis. The episode resembles a mythical tale; Oedipus has quite rightly been invoked in connection with it.[48] But this comparison points to the importance of the victim as scapegoat, not merely a simple caricature of the myth.[49] Zadig's return to Babylon takes place in a setting of pervasive crisis. All the ancient quarrels seem to be raging in the town where he is soon to be proclaimed king. Moabdar's death has divided the country, which is in the grip of civil conflict: "Everything is in confusion in Babylon"; "Babylon is one big nest of cutthroats. . . . the empire is laid waste" (384). The battles that Zadig must face mimic this crisis; they dramatize the rivalries that imperil the community. The crown is not only what is at stake in the competition, but it is also a sort of simulacrum of the victim; it is supposed to polarize all desires. Whoever wins the crown will necessarily occupy the place of the sacred, given the level of prowess expected from the winner and the initiation process the community requires him to undergo. Through his victory, Zadig occupies this place as his own; with him he brings a remedy for the people's vengeance.[50] We can no longer see the ending of *Zadig* simply as the sudden victory of wisdom over the violence of superstition, as the dawn of the utopian kingdom of justice to come and the appearance of history.[51] It is henceforth crucial to acknowledge the victimlike mechanism through which this renaissance takes shape. The effect of Zadig's enlightenment is to repel a vast archaic realm: an underlayer of wars, diverse polemics, mutually hateful beliefs. If the king institutes historical society, it is by resolving conflicts through his person, by relegating to the past the divisions that threaten collective homogeneity.

At the center of his story Voltaire intentionally placed an envious rival of Zadig's—Arimaze, the philosopher's thwarted double. The rival embodies the mimetic evil that afflicts our societies and from which we must free ourselves at all cost. At the end of *Zadig*, Arimaze dies by his own evil: "The Envious died of rage and shame" (412). Reason will triumph over the prevailing state of murder and warring customs. At the end of the story, violence— the negative principle—is also mastered. The bandit Arbogad is recuperated into Zadig's army. The royal crown not only unifies power but also takes force in hand. Let us not forget that the conciliatory philosopher takes the place of an assassinated monarch. Such is his precarious state of happiness.

The Trials and Tribulations of Candide

In its own fashion, *Candide* narrates the same story as *Zadig*. Candide's journey through life is also a sacrificial one.[52] Here, too, a Providentialist interpretation suppresses the mimetic structuring of the text. In this parodic dramatization of "the best of all possible worlds,"[53] a string of absurd catastrophes does not merely give the lie to a Leibnizian reading; more important, at each stop on his journey Candide confronts collective violence, the hostile reciprocity of human relations. The devil dwells in the world and people are wolves to one another. The anthropic relation is, in fact, an animal one.[54] The gift is unknown to people; their symmetrical relation to their neighbors operates solely through aggression and force. Voltaire shows how contagious, absurd, and insane this relationship is. It is in culture that this degradation of nature into violent animality is found in its most sophisticated and yet deplorable forms: "Men . . . must have corrupted nature a little, for they were not born wolves, and they have become wolves. God did not give them twenty-four-pounder cannons or bayonets, and they have made bayonets and cannons to destroy each other" (239).

Free-floating war—such appears to be the vocation of *homo lupus*, thus the sequence of wars of every kind punctuating this tale. This is the last phase in collective degradation. I believe that the physical catastrophes must be read in the same way. They conceal the same collective violence, the chaos of the mob; it is not incidental that the narrative moves from an earthquake to a plague. These natural phenomena must be considered from an anthropological standpoint: they are not so much the mark of the world's chaotic absurdity as they are manifestations of a social state doomed to violence and undifferentiation.[55] In other words, the physical disorder of the world imitates the disorder of its human population. The space in *Candide* is complex, tortured, overpopulated. The terrain is dangerous and turbulent (earthquakes, ship-wrecking seas, escarpments), but the turbulence of human multitudes—*turba*—is ubiquitous (disorderly crowds, armies, pirates, thieves): "A million drilled assassins go from one end of Europe to the other murdering and robbing with discipline in order to earn their bread" (287).

In the midst of these events, Candide's role is that of the chosen victim. His place in the tale seems to allow him no other fate. His presence alone is sometimes enough to unleash a whole series of catastrophes. With the effect of a sort of evil eye, he seems to bring evil with him wherever he goes. This is precisely what happens to Candide in Lisbon, where he is chosen as one of the victims responsible for the earthquake in order to ward off the possibility of further calamity.[56]

In Eldorado—the utopia that Voltaire sets up at the center of *Candide*, nestled in an artificial valley of peace midway between the primitive world and the garden—the violence of others has been driven beyond the borders, excluded from this physical space. Eldorado's enclosure, its inaccessible perimeters, bar European savagery and the old relations of an inadmissible world: "We are surrounded by inaccessible rocks and precipices, we have hitherto been exempt from the rapacity of the nations of Europe who have an inconceivable lust for the pebbles and mud of our land

and would kill us to the last man to get possession of them" (276). Rugged landscape and violent people are also equated elsewhere in the text, when Cacambo and Candide draw near Cayenne: "Mountains, rivers, precipices, brigands, and savages were everywhere terrible obstacles" (272).

Eldorado's peace seems completely artificial. If competition has been eliminated, if the law has been internalized, and if respect for the other reigns supreme, we do not know at what price these conditions have been achieved. This oasis of peace in the midst of the world's turbulence is impossible, and Candide is not long in leaving it behind.

The European world is characterized by the same negative multiplicity. The niceties of civilization only thinly conceal the same savagery that is found among the aggregates of primitive times. Hence Paris is "a chaos, a throng" (289). The social space has become a stage for war: "All the rest of their time is passed in senseless quarrels: Jansenists with Molinists, lawyers with churchmen, men of letters with men of letters, courtiers with courtiers, financiers with the people, wives with husbands, relatives with relatives—'tis an eternal war" (296). The primitive world is no longer the only one overwhelmed by the evil of rivalry; it could even be said that such evil, effectively transformed, is more at home in conditions of civil peace:

> ... I confess that when I consider this globe, or rather this globule, I think that God has abandoned it to some evil creature—always excepting Eldorado. I have never seen a town which did not desire the ruin of the next town, never a family which did not wish to exterminate some other family. ... and in the towns which seem to enjoy peace and where the arts flourish, men are devoured by more envy, troubles, and worries than the afflictions of a besieged town. (287)

This account is not so far removed from the symmetrical and undifferentiated space that Voltaire describes at the beginning of the story in the episode pitting the Abarians against the Bulgarians. All the figures of impurity were already present then: women butchered, girls raped, senseless killings. Violent reciprocity is rampant: "It was an Abare village which the Bulgarians had burned. ... Candide fled to another village as fast as he could; it belonged to the Bulgarians, and Abarian heroes had treated it in the same way" (234–35). Voltaire expresses similar scorn in the *Philosophical Dictionary* when he writes that war is "this universal rage which devours the world."[57]

The Garden

The garden, the hastily concocted philosophical response that brings the story to a conclusion, might offer us a possible alternative to such scenarios of violence. A whole slew of dated hermeneutics have been invoked in attempts to bury the virtues of this garden: literary history, which conceives of it as a response to the illogic of Providence; Marxist interpretations, which see it as a cogent precursor to communism (human beings joining forces to take charge of their destiny founded on a new basis of exchange); and existentialism, which finds the garden an absurd response to the absurdity of existence. In my opinion, however, the originality of the alternative that is represented by the garden must be understood against the double backdrop of the primitive world described at the beginning (wars, plagues, and brigandage) and of competitive European society.

True, the garden has the appearance of an individualist choice. But it is offered as an alternative form of sociality. Work as a ritual will put an end to collective violence by exercising individual talents for the good of the community. The new culture of Candide's garden is one of service to the collective. The garden is, in fact, a copy of the one inhabited by the wise Turk whom Candide encountered on the road to the little farm. By retreating to his garden, the Turk avoids the violence of history: he distances himself from human exchange, the competitive market. His Epicurean retreat is a family household, a group of close friends: "His two daughters and his two sons presented them with several kinds of sherbet which they made themselves, caymac flavored with candied citron peel, oranges, lemons, limes, pineapples, dates, pistachios, and Mocha coffee" (326). They spend no more time in Constantinople than what is necessary to sell what has been produced at home. Thus competition is avoided, along with all the corruptions of the mercantile arena. Far removed from other men, the sage is also oblivious to their old ambitions: "I presume that in general those who meddle with public affairs sometimes perish miserably." So he avoids politics: "I have never known the name of any mufti or of any vizier" (326).

The intervention of the idea of monarchy seems to lead back to the practice of sacrifice. How else can one explain the list of regicides that precedes the ultimate choice of the garden? (Or the famous supper of fallen kings gathered together in Venice for the carnival?) Here is the astonishing list that Voltaire gives us to read:

> Eglon, King of the Moabites, was murdered by Ehud; Absalom was hanged by the hair and pierced by three darts; King Nadab, son of Jeroboam, was killed by Baasha; King Elah by Zimri; Ahaziah by Jehu; Athaliah by Jehoiada; the Kings Jehoiakim, Jeconiah, and Zedekiah were made slaves. You know in what manner died Croesus, Astyages, Darious, Denys of Syracuse, Pyrrhus, Perseus, Hannibal, Jugurtha, Ariovistus, Caesar, Pompey, Nero, Otho, Vitellius, Domitian, Richard II of England, Edward II, Henry VI, Richard III, Mary Stuart, Charles I, the three Henrys of France, the Emperor Henry IV. You know . . . (326)

Oddly enough, Candide wishes to efface this vengeful knowledge with his horticultural alternative: "'I also know,' said Candide, 'that we should cultivate our gardens'" (327). It is around the figure of Candide (in a movement that paradoxically recalls the function of the sovereign) that the peaceful community organizes itself. The sudden turnaround Candide evinces can be easily explained if we adopt a ritual perspective. The ancient victim, the bastard of the narrative, whom Voltaire has made white (the very etymology of his name conveys his candor), is now capable in his desire to forget of putting an end to hostilities. At the close of the story, he eliminates the baron's son, the twin brother of violence.[58] He becomes a political model of the Good Shepherd. Michel Foucault rightly perceived the sacred function of the Shepherd-King in the genealogy of political power: his role consists in pacifying hostilities within the polis. Even if in Plato the pastoral function of the political leader is defined in contradistinction to the doctor or farmer, the proximity of these ritualistic and curative functions to the métier of the king is evident. The royal art of reigning can be compared to that of the weaver in a metaphor for the ritual unification of the community: "Thus to weave 'the most magnificent of all fabrics.' The whole population, 'slaves and freemen, wrapped up in its folds.'"[59]

Jacques van den Heuvel has rightly detected a mystical compo-nent in the little farm on the shores of the Propontis.[60] But the only evidence that could support such an intuition is the pacify-ing effect of the work ritual. The new culture also brings about social harmony through daily activities—weaving, embroidery, tapestry, pastry making—whose full ritualistic significance must be recognized; murderous, competitive, rivalrous history is thereby expelled. The time for murders and sacrificed kings has passed. Agriculture is foundation, alliance; here, peace of the garden has returned, by the shores of the river, amongst friends: "We must cultivate our gardens" (328). Candide's philosophical injunction should be understood as an ingenious invention. It presents a third way, an alternative to the rival philosophies of Pangloss (optimism) and Martin (pessimism). It has the force of reason; it leaves aside metaphysics; it forges benevolent reciprocity, a new way of relating to the beings and objects of the world.

Work is the primary cause of all the troubles, tribulations, and worries of humankind. Voltaire looks to rites to find the origin of work, which he invents as a sacrificial solution.[61] One must be of service, according to the story. The garden enjoins an exchange of tasks that keeps competition at bay. The new kind of relation proposed by the garden must be seen as an autonomist impera-tive. Candide suggests that we should forget metaphysical argu-ments that are incapable of justifying our destiny. From now on, the forging of destiny will be a joint project. The new order founded by the garden is the sum of each person's interests. "The little farm yielded well" (327): in a sense, this is its rational econ-omy. This proposition brings to mind Michel Serres's garden in *La naissance de la physique* (The birth of physics). Here, too, the minimum is sought as an escape from violent history and poli-tics. Serres writes: "To be satisfied with the limited. To build one's nest close by the incipient, little garden where fig trees grow"; "Epicurean secession, dissidence and retreat through peaceful practices, serenity, withdrawal as far as possible from violence and death. Which is to say, or almost to say, that just beyond one's borders, outside the garden, the battle rages and the plague litters the forum with corpses."[62] The institution of the garden in *Candide* signals the end of the wanton expenditure both of violence and of the artificial goods of Eldorado, now con-

signed to the economy of the real world. Like an asylum, this cor-
ner of the world has left far behind it the unending succession of
sacrifices, the violence of the wolf-men. But these may come back
to haunt this "little" society, like the shadows of a story not so
long gone:

> From the windows of the farm they often watched the ships going
> by, filled with effendis, pashas, and cadis, who were being exiled to
> Lemnos, to Mitylene and Erzerum. They saw other cadis, other
> pashas, and other effendis coming back to take the place of the ex-
> iles and to be exiled in their turn. They saw the neatly impaled
> heads which were taken to the Sublime Porte. (324)

Voltaire offers two solutions to human violence. The first,
Zadig, institutes history and puts an end to anarchic violence: it
is judicial. The second, *Candide*, has already retreated from history itself; ritualistic and purgative, it is ultimately oblivious to
the murderous repetition of history.[63]

3 / The Order of Evils[1] (Rousseau)

In his *Confessions*, Rousseau writes of "wandering deep into the forest" for the sojourn that resulted in his *Discourse on the Origin and Foundations of Inequality among Men* (1755):

> I sought and I found the vision of those primitive times, the history of which I proudly traced. I demolished the petty lies of mankind; I dared to strip man's nature naked, to follow the progress of time, and trace the things which have distorted it; and by comparing man as he has made himself with man as he is by nature I showed him in his pretended perfection the true source of his misery.[2]

In order to write the *Discourse*, Rousseau went into isolation in the forest of Saint-Germain for eight days of penitence. He left behind the city, with its prestigious academies and glorious passions, in order to conjure up the unfolding drama of origins, to revive the script of primitive times. This sylvan retreat from worldly life was essential to Rousseau's contemplation of the wretched procession of human progress, like a dying man watching his life pass before his eyes in a turbulent film. Yet in a sense Rousseau's modus operandi was already deceptively oblique. Though he was fleeing from the city and men, what he sought in the echoing woods was the respect of none other than the academicians. The forest where Jean-Jacques cloistered himself retained only the lingering scent of its origins. A warehouse stockpiled with images of its own past, it reverberated with concepts; it had become the idea of itself. It was in vain that Rousseau sought the men of ages past here. The dense shadows of the forest sent him back to his writing page where he would rediscover the masks of his own age.

Genesis

To convey human decadence, Rousseau is fond of employing images of corruption, of corrosion devastating the original state. The powerful image that begins the second *Discourse* has often been commented on. This image of the statue of Glaucus—a god monstrously disfigured through the effects of time and the force of storms[3]—illustrates the way civilized man appears to Rousseau: oddly "ravaged" by the weight of the years, carried away by the passions that distance him from his childhood. Primitive man has been buried under layers of sedimentation, which have left him disfigured. All that remains is his monstrous modernity. How does Rousseau explain this metamorphosis? How did man get here from there?

First, there are physical, chance causes that divide the human band into two groups: one will embark on an evolutionary path, straying further and further from its natural prototype; the other will instead remain stagnant, remaining by this very "virtue" closer to its origins. But this mode of evolution is quickly set aside by Rousseau, who goes on to offer a complicated genealogy of the passions that are responsible for corrupting man's heart permanently. This is what I would like to analyze by tracing the virtual, fictive anthropology that appears to be contained in the *Discourse*.

During the perfection of primitive times natural man has already given evidence of an original evil, which Rousseau does not seem to want to acknowledge (or, rather, which he will shift to a later stage, as men are not yet living in groups). This evil consists in man's mimeticism, his imitative capacity, which is brought to bear from the beginning—not in relation to his fellow men but in relation to those creatures that are the farthest removed from him, the animals. In fact, we see the first signs of the progress of human intelligence in the primary identifications of this initial specular episode: "Men, dispersed among the animals, observe and imitate their industry, and thereby raise themselves to the level of animal instinct" (40). Man's paucity of instinct, his original deprivation, propels him into a sort of pluralized mimeticism. Not only does he imitate the animals; he also acquires the diverse instincts of different species. Rousseau insists on this original human dispossession: "Man, who may perhaps have [no instinct] that belongs to him, appropriates all of them to himself, feeds himself equally well on most of the various foods which the other animals divide among themselves" (40). In the civil state, man's voracity will be directed against his fellow man (*semblable*) in a relationship implying similarity and comparison; it is the result of his excessive dependence. Rousseau decries the mimetic cannibalism that people exhibit: "We who can no longer get along without devouring men."[4]

In one of the famous notes that are particular to the second *Discourse*, Rousseau seems to envision a possible alteration of natural man. Before becoming carnivorous, this natural being must have been frugivorous; Rousseau invokes the configuration of the teeth and intestines as proof. This is a crucial point: as long as a vegetarian diet is sufficient, man is able to maintain his natural isolation, whereas the need for meat immediately introduces competition, the desire to obtain the same object: "For since prey is nearly the exclusive subject of fighting among carnivorous animals, and since frugivorous animals live among themselves in continual peace, if the human species were of this latter genus, it is clear that it would have had a much easier time subsisting in the state of nature, and much less need and occasion to leave it" (86–87). Rousseau would like to believe that man is naturally weak and peaceful. But what has happened is that man has substituted skill and cleverness for the brute strength that he lacks. Let us not forget that his most immediate competitors are not yet other men but, rather, animals. Rousseau would like to deny the existence of a natural instinct for violence in human beings and animals alike, but a competitive instinct, the drive for comparison, permeates his descriptions: "But since a savage man lives dispersed among the animals and, finding himself early on in a position to measure himself against them, he soon makes the comparison; and, aware that he surpasses them in skillfulness more than they surpass him in strength, he learns not to fear them any more" (41).

Later in the course of evolution, when people come to confront others of their kind, the shift to force as the sole means of mediation emerges as the source of all social ills. Peaceful imitation of animals degenerates into real fighting. Competition loses all moderation and benign neighborly relations rapidly vanish. Humanity is infected with the virus of superiority, and animals are the first rivals and victims: "He trained himself to set traps for them; he *tricked* them in a thousand different ways. And although several surpassed him in fighting strength or in swiftness in running, of those that could serve him or hurt him, he became in time the master of the former and the scourge of the latter" (61; emphasis added). This early field of confrontation is man's training ground. It will not be long before, in his first associations with others, he will reproduce these newly acquired violent gestures that he has developed with animals. The learning of relationality takes place through the mediation of force. Inexorably, relation itself becomes a relation of competition: "Everyone sought to obtain his own advantage, either by overt force, if he believed he could, or by cleverness and cunning, if he felt himself to be the weaker" (62).

Yet Rousseau persists in denying man's original violence and his savagery in the state of nature; he disagrees with Hobbes on this particular point. Rousseau views fraternal violence—violence perpetrated among close relatives—as one of the British philosopher's various inventions:

> The evil man [says Hobbes] is a robust child. It remains to be seen whether savage man is a robust child. Were we to grant him this, what would we conclude from it? That if this man were as dependent on others when he is robust as he is when he is weak, there is no type of excess to which he would not tend: he would beat his mother if she were too slow in offering him her breast; he would strangle one of his younger brothers, should he find him annoying; he would bite the other brother's leg. (53)

Similarly, Rousseau considers that in the state of nature vengeance remains a purely reactive gesture, unmeditated, not caught up in a psychological relationship with the other. It is a matter of immediate physical contact: man reacted "right then and there, like the dog that bites the stone that is thrown at him" (55). In the civil state, on the other hand—but only at its beginnings among the first tentative glimmers of the idea of justice—vengeance appears instead as a supplement to physical violence, a deferred expression of outrage. It is now a form of reasoning, of reflecting (on) the offense; it becomes an insult. Vengeance has turned into reciprocal offense. Now violence has taken on the face of the other, and along with it that other's complex share of mimetic interferences—vanity, respect, esteem, and scorn. One's neighbor has become a menacing obstacle.

It is now possible to discern Rousseau's anthropology, which might in some sense be termed an anthropology of communication. In this system, imitation (of the other) functions as the originating generative faculty. Paraphrasing Lévi-Strauss, we might say that Rousseau is the most anthropological of the *philosophes*.[5] More than Voltaire or even Montesquieu, Rousseau attempts to locate a theoretical essence in the discipline of anthropology, developing a system of thought to which he gives axiological coherence. In sum, then, man starts out in isolation. Then, in a mounting process of individualization, he begins to identify with animal species: he, too, becomes a member of a herd. The first steps toward socialization are marked by imitative beginnings. If we are to understand Rousseau's sociology, we must fully admit the concept of imitation as the source of human evil. His interpreters have generally preferred to stop at neighboring or derivative concepts that were later to serve in constructing the thought of the individual: *amour-propre* (vanity, pride, egocentrism) and *amour de soi* (love of self, self-interest, self-preservation).[6] Rousseau, it must be said, remains the most incontestably modern thinker of all the *philosophes* by virtue of the radical negativity with which he invests his concepts of sociability. Without Rousseau, it would be impossible to understand Hegel, Jean-Paul Sartre, or any of the other philosophers who posit alterity—or otherness—as the major problem of subjectivity.

Mimesis, for example, governs the origin of property. Rousseau's argument is faultless: the strongest men are the first ones to construct dwellings for themselves. In order to avoid potential disputes, the weakest agree to imitate them. Rousseau makes every effort to separate competition from the state of nature. His fiction of origins must remain pure. Competition can only take shape on the verge of decadence; it provokes the fall of man into the civil state. Only at this stage is man's imitative nature deployed. Or, rather, this is the moment when imitation becomes harmful. Indeed, Rousseau writes in *Emile* that "man is an imitator. Even animals are. The taste for imitation belongs to well-ordered nature; but in a society it degenerates into vice"; "the foundation of imitation among us comes from the desire always to be transported out of ourselves."[7]

My project here is to expose the foundations of Rousseau's hypothesis and to show how he manages to reject the primary ambivalence of imitation and thereby skirt around the original violence of human beings. In one passage, for example, the author of the second *Discourse* can be caught in a flagrantly arbitrary theoretical manipulation in connection with the division of the sexes. In order to forestall the idea of rivalry—of jealousy between males vying for the same female body—Rousseau declares that the female population is anything but scarce; clearly, then, it makes no sense to envision violent competition over the same object. In the state of nature, Rousseau maintains, "the number of females generally surpasses the number of males, and . . . human females, unlike those of other species, have never been observed to have periods of heat and exclusion" (57). Jealousy is a recent development: the perversity of civilized man has produced jealous lovers and vengeful spouses who engage in duels and murders.

On the basis of this example we might generalize as follows: in the state of nature, man does not know objects; he is ruled by need. Or, rather, let us say that his relation to the object is unmediated. The object, which is consumed in an instant, can be said to have an existence only during the instant in which the feeling of need for it arises. Desire operates quite differently. In the case of desire, an object emits a persistent glow. It is suspended somehow outside the field of need; its consumption is deferred. It is of interest only inasmuch as it is coveted by the other, and the greater the number of people who are interested in it, the more desirable it is. Mediation (the marking of the object by the desire of the other) has replaced the unmediated relation. The being that desires corresponds to man in the civil state. Rousseau claims that perfectibility is the evil at the root of all the rest. Yet it is no doubt the distance at which the object is held that engenders all ills. The state of nature supposed a coincidence of passions and needs (Rousseau even says at times that natural man has neither needs nor passions). In the civil state, we see this mechanism perverted: passions are directed no longer toward needs, but toward the passions of others or, rather, passions mimic other people's needs. Needs thus become superfluous, and henceforth all is given over to representation, to display: "The less natural and pressing the needs, the more the passions increase" (91). The reign of envy, competition, jealousy, and rivalries is established. Man has shifted from goods to signs, to the representation of wealth—in short, to universal covetousness.

The origin of languages is governed by a similar process. A language participates in the new dignity of the object. The language does not communicate the need for the other (a gesture is sufficient for that). In language the object becomes an alibi, communicating the desire to enter into a relation; it is the mediator of a relation. The *Essay on the Origin of Languages* offers a few specific examples. The object as a need is always averted, seduced, in the service of specular shock, of the ecstasy of communication: "The first tongues, children of pleasure rather than need, long bore the mark of their father. They lost their seductive tone with the advent of feelings to which they had given birth, when new needs arose among men, forcing each to be mindful only of his own welfare, and to withdraw his heart into himself."[8] The first groupings of men are marked by this disappearance of the object, by the vanishing of the era of need. In fact, the more the object seems to indicate need, the more it becomes a sign of desire. The object categorically deceives. Rousseau choreographs this moment in a delightful scene: "Imperceptibly, water becomes more necessary. The livestock become thirsty more often. One would arrive in haste and leave with regret . . . the only measure of time would be the alternation of amusement and boredom. . . . Little by little they become less shy with each other. In trying to make oneself understood, one learns to explain oneself."[9] The originary metaphor bears the mark of this extraordinary confrontation with the other. In the case of metaphor, the sign loses sight of the real object; it is imbued with the presence of the other. Jacques Derrida was right to see the metaphor as passionate, emotional.[10]

The chief example in the *Essay on the Origin of Languages* is the case of fear:

> Upon meeting others, a savage man will initially be frightened. Because of his fear he sees the others as bigger and stronger than himself. He calls them *giants*. After many experiences, he recognizes that these so-called giants are neither bigger nor stronger than he. Their stature does not approach the idea he had initially attached to the word giant. So he invents another name common to them and to him, such as the name *man*, for example, and leaves *giant* to the fictitious object that had impressed him during his illusion. That is how the figurative word is born before the literal word, when our gaze is held in passionate fascination; and how it is that the first idea it conveys to us is not that of the truth.[11]

In *Of Grammatology*, in which Derrida is almost exclusively concerned with the question of writing, he makes this dazzling remark on the fear generated by the gaze of the other:

> Does the example of fear come by chance? Does not the metaphoric origin of language lead us necessarily to a situation of threat, distress, and dereliction, to an archaic solitude, to the anguish of dispersion? Absolute fear would then be the first encounter of the other as *other:* as other than I and as other than itself. I can answer the threat of the other as other (than I) only by transforming it into another (than itself), through altering it in my imagination, my fear, or my desire.[12]

Later, when Rousseau attempts to conceive of an unmediated relation with the object, he must make *jouissance* and desire coincide in a single impulse of compensation, yet he must also assure himself of his jealous possession: "Removing from the object everything that is foreign to his covetousness, [the imagination] presents it to him only as suited to his desire in all respects."[13] Rousseau's aim is, in fact, less to capture the object than to limn the contours of the self faced with the anguishing loss of self-possession.

When he looks at the object, Rousseau sees double. If he goes out of his way to isolate the object in its purity, it is because he perceives the violence of desires that lurks at the origin of property. The object is always already usurped by the other. When Rousseau arrives at the property formula in the second *Discourse*—the impulse to claim that "this belongs to me"—he has made a giant leap in understanding this original act of violence. The birth of property is indeed marked by this vital intuition: it is an advance gained over the other's desire (for the object).[14]

An even more critical degradation affects another crucial concept in the second *Discourse*, that of *amour de soi*, which in the civil state is transformed into *amour-propre*. *Amour de soi*, which dictates the behavior of natural man, corresponds to the state of man in isolation; it metamorphoses into *amour-propre* when the other appears on the horizon. *Amour-propre* turns man into a relational being. Rousseau draws these crucial distinctions:

> We must not confuse egocentrism [*amour-propre*] with love of oneself [*amour de soi*], two passions very different by virtue of both their nature and their effects. Love of oneself is a natural sentiment which moves every animal to be vigilant in its own preservation and which, directed in man by reason and modified by pity, produces humanity and virtue. Egocentrism is merely a sentiment that is relative, artificial and born in society, which moves each individual to value himself more than anyone else, which inspires in men all the evils they cause one another, and which is the true source of honor.
>
> . . . in our primitive state, in the veritable state of nature, egocentrism does not exist; for since each particular man regards himself as the only spectator who observes him, as the only being in the universe that takes an interest in him, as the only judge of his own merit, it is impossible that a sentiment which has its source in comparisons that he is not in a position to make could germinate in his soul. (106)

Amour-propre is in fact disguised as narcissism: what appears to be the individual's own self-preoccupation is really intended for the other's contemplation. *Amour-propre* is pervaded by an awareness of the other: this is the source of its most woeful decadence. In a sense, *amour-propre* is *amour de soi* transformed into an obscene representation of itself.

Rousseau says that *amour de soi* is what generates pity. But when we read the definitions of pity, it becomes evident that it contains the seeds of its own corruption. Pity requires self-exteriorization; it necessitates identification with the other, putting one "in the position of the one who suffers" (54). But Rousseau adds that pity effects an ersatz movement of the self toward the other. There is identification with the other, but the identification loops back to the self—it is a false move. If we put ourselves in the place of the other, it is through an excessive identification with ourselves. Derrida underscores this paradox: "The more you identify with the other, the better you feel his suffering as *his:* our own suffering is that of the other. That of the other, as itself, must remain the other's. There is no authentic identification except in a certain non-identification."[15] In the *Discourse,* Rousseau says clearly that identification with the other "must have been infinitely closer in the state of nature" (54). The civil state brings about the utter corruption of this principle. Pity made it possible to identify positively with the other, since it was through the other that the subject "projected" his own preservation. In the civil state, the advent of interests causes this feeling to be left behind. The desire for self-preservation is accompanied by a wish to annihilate the other. Death, feared with respect to oneself, is now desired for others: "We find our advantage in the setbacks of our fellow-men"; "each finds his profit in the misfortune of another" (90). Rousseau's thought in this regard is neatly summed up in a definition that appears in *Rousseau, Judge of Jean-Jacques.* He describes the violent transformation of *amour de soi* into *amour-propre,* the metamorphosis of the object of need into the object of envy and the appearance of the rival:

> The primitive passions, which all tend directly toward our happiness, focus us only on objects that relate to it, and having only the love of self [*amour de soi*] as a principle, are all loving and gentle in their essence. But when they are deflected from their object by obstacles, they are focused on removing the obstacle rather than reaching the object; then they change nature and become irascible and hateful. And this is how the love of self, which is a good and absolute feeling, becomes amour-propre; which is to say a relative feeling by which one makes comparison; the latter feeling demands preferences, whose enjoyment is purely negative, and it no longer seeks satisfaction in our own benefit, but solely in the harm of another.[16]

Jean Starobinski was particularly fascinated by the term *obstacle,* which for him captured something mysterious about Rousseau's text.[17] In the passage just cited, the obstacle is clearly the rival, the other—the one intervening between the subject and the object. The obstacle is what desire stumbles into; it is the site of interacting desires. The gaze is no longer fixed solely on the object; it is crossed, intercepted by the gaze of the other. Man will never recover from this fascination, from this originary seduction. At the same time the obstacle is none other than the scandal (*skandalon*), the stumbling block—man's original sin. The religious connotation of the term must not be allowed to obscure the mechanical definition that Rousseau gives it:

> All the first movements of nature are good and right. They aim as directly as possible toward our preservation and our happiness, but soon lacking strength to maintain their original direction through so much resistance, they let themselves be deflected by a thousand obstacles which, turning them away from their true goal, make them take oblique paths where man forgets his original destination.[18]

Through this natural deficiency the face of the other is revealed. Derrida would say that the other is the supplement of origin.

In order to uphold the benevolent activity of pity, Rousseau indicates the difference between pity and envy—at the cost, however, of a number of paradoxes. He writes in *Emile:*

> Pity is sweet because, in putting ourselves in the place of the one who suffers, we nevertheless feel the pleasure of not suffering as he does. Envy is bitter because the sight of a happy man, far from putting the envious man in his place, makes the envious man regret not being there. It seems that the one exempts us from the ills he suffers, and the other takes from us the goods he enjoys.[19]

The envious subject is turned back on his own unhappy condition. In this sense, identification through envy is invidious—utterly destructive.

The Violence of Theater

The degradation of pity in the civil order dominates Rousseau's entire critique of the theater. In the *Discourse,* Rousseau explains pity by establishing a theatrical mechanism, a space of representation: "Commiseration will be all the more energetic as the witnessing animal identifies itself more intimately with the suffering animal" (54). In the *Essay on the Origin of Languages,* Rousseau describes the phenomenon more fully, specifying the role that imagination plays in it: "We suffer only as much as we believe him to suffer. It is not in ourselves, but in him that we suffer"; Rousseau calls this identification a form of transport.[20] The pitying subject is literally altered. A transference of emotions must take place between the spectator and the suffering animal. Rousseau could not have chosen a more apt word than *compassion*. To identify with the other means to experience his passion. In order to understand what transpires at the theater, we must undertake a detailed reading of the argument in the *Letter to M. d'Alembert on the Theatre.*

To begin, the problem of the theater is that it facilitates a false convergence of emotions. The theater may well be defined as "a painting of the human passions," but these passions are "repulsive passions," simulacra of emotions, "the original of which is in every heart."[21] The theater trades in cheap, gaudy emotions. It is wrong, according to Rousseau, to believe in the cathartic power of theater to expunge passions. The business of the theater is, on the contrary, to create passions. The false object of representation touches the spectators to the point of causing a previously unknown emotion to take shape in them. Theatrical mimesis affects spectators to such an extent that they may relive the passions *après coup*, in a deferred action, and this very repetition constitutes an occasion for genuine pleasure:

> Do the emotion, the disturbance, and the softening which are felt within oneself and which continue after the play give indication of an immediate disposition to master and regulate our passions? Are the lively and touching impressions to which we become accustomed and which return so often, quite the means to moderate our sentiments in the case of need? Why should the image of the sufferings born of the passions efface that of the transports of pleasure and joy which are also seen to be born of them? (21)

The ambivalence of identification in the case of the theater is most clearly denounced when Rousseau examines the outcome of pity. In pity born of the theater, the spectator does away with actual suffering; he suffers by proxy. The other's misfortune is contaminated by representation: this separates theatrical pity from natural pity, in which actor and spectator are intimately joined. In the theater, identification with a sufferer costs us nothing. Rousseau insists on the fact that we escape virtually scot-free. He gives the example of tragedy:

> I hear it said that tragedy leads to pity through fear. So it does; but what is pity? A fleeting and vain emotion which lasts no longer than

the illusion which produced it; a vestige of natural sentiment soon stifled by the passions; a sterile pity which feeds on a few tears and which has never produced the slightest act of humanity. Thus, the sanguinary Sulla cried at the account of evils he had not himself committed. Thus, the tyrant of Phera hid himself at the theatre for fear of being seen groaning with Andromache and Priam, while he heard without emotion the cries of so many unfortunate victims slain daily by his orders. . . .

If, according to the observation of Diogenes Laertius, the heart is more readily touched by feigned ills than real ones, if theatrical imitations draw forth more tears than would the presence of the objects imitated, it is less because the emotions are feebler and do not reach the level of pain, as the Abbé du Bos believes, than because they are pure and without mixture of anxiety for ourselves. In giving our tears to these fictions, we have satisfied all the rights of humanity without having to give anything more of ourselves. (24–25)

At bottom, the problem is even more serious. A premium of narcissistic pleasure always enters into theatrical pity. It is true that natural pity already contains the seeds of a certain egotistical pleasure, a self-satisfaction: "Pity is such a delightful sentiment that it is not surprising that one seeks to experience it."[22] The problem is that theater itself is seductive; representation fascinates and charms.[23] Rousseau foregrounds the quality of speech and the arrangement of the scenes among the major elements of this seduction. Theatrical contagion stems from the image itself, with its mimetic monopoly and the force of its appeal. The spectator generally wishes to repeat the affective experience that was produced during the performance. *Après coup,* the spectator fantasizes about the emotion: "The sweet emotions that are felt are not in themselves a definite object, but they produce the need for one" (51). This reproach, leveled against the representation of love, applies equally to tragedy. In tragedy it is crime instead that seduces. Idealized, embellished crime wields the indelible power of the image.

The violence of theater resides in its persuasive force. It is significant that Rousseau chooses to discuss Voltaire's *Mahomet* among other contemporary plays. In Rousseau's mind, the moral ambiguity of the play lies in the message that, despite the author's critical intention, fanaticism is seductive. Mahomet is portrayed as larger than life; he inspires terror and wonder. Rousseau is worried about the effect of the prophet's "greatness of soul" on the characters (31). In other words, Rousseau fears not so much the denunciation of fanaticism as its affective charge, its persuasive explosiveness.

Festivals and Tribunals

The theater is not in a position to correct manners and morals. On the contrary, it incites passions, inflames the audience, encourages vice, and idealizes violence. In the plays he chose to comment on in his *Letter to M. d'Alembert*, Rousseau points out the incessant victimization of virtue: the character who is supposed to represent this moral sentiment is never able to achieve idealization, does not invite benevolent identification, and does not have the resources of the model to be imitated. Such is the case with Alceste in *The Misanthrope* and with Titus in *Berenice*: both characters are sacrificed at the altar of passion. To the extent that the theatre does not edify or rectify morals, Rousseau judges it irrefragably reprehensible. With what, then, should it be replaced in the polis?

Rousseau proposes festivals as a substitute. If theater prevents real identification with the actor's suffering (and through him, with the character he portrays), and if, above all, the efficacy of theatrical identification is nil, this flaw must be remedied in the conception of the festival. All that needs to be done is to facilitate mimesis, to multiply its specular effects to the point of saturation: "Let the spectators become an entertainment to themselves; make them actors themselves; do it so that each sees and loves himself in the others so that all will be better united" (126). The general will is thus experienced by means of contagion, positive interidentification, pure emotional reciprocity. This experience is what Jean Starobinski refers to as "transparency" in *Jean-Jacques Rousseau: Transparency and Obstruction.*

It seems to me, on a closer reading, that the festive relation also functions differently. The reversibility alluded to above is not perfect. There is reciprocal identification, but it occurs in relation to an external model. Into the midst of the festival and its supposed equality, Rousseau introduces competition or specular conflict. The examples of public festivals that he favors include public prize giving: "Every year we have reviews, public prizes, kings of the harquebus, the cannon, and sailing . . . of such kings there cannot be too many. . . . Why should we not found, on the model of the military prizes, other prizes for gymnastics, wrestling, running, discus, and the various bodily exercises?" (126–27). The object of the festival, even though it is symbolic, appears in all its mediating force, fomenting the reciprocal struggle of like against like: "Could there be an entertainment in the world more brilliant than seeing, on this vast and superb body of water, hundreds of boats, elegantly equipped, starting together at the given signal to go and capture a flag planted at the finish, then serving as a cortege for the victor returning in triumph to receive his well-earned prize?" (127). Rousseau insists on the homogenizing virtues of the festival: "All the societies constitute but one, all become common to all." (127). But out of this unanimity, one might say, certain members of the community end up feeling excluded. The whole strategy of prizes and contests is meant to polarize the participants toward a single goal, a shared desire; but the moment will come in which the equilibrium is shattered. At this point a difference is produced: it is the moment of the most beautiful, or the strongest, and so forth. Nor should we hesitate to read in the titles that are accorded to the winners—king and queen—echos of violent rituals. In his essay on the government of Poland, Rousseau proposes that the Polish adopt games modeled on ancient combats and tournaments, which he sees as veritable "arenas of honor and competition. . . . with, as in the past, honors and prizes for the victors."[24]

Among these various festivals, one type in particular has caught the attention of commentators; Rousseau grants it pride of place at the end of his letter. The balls where matches are made among the marriageable young do not escape specular contagion any more than other festivals. Such balls exude no less conflict and rivalry. Once again, Rousseau imposes emulation and distinction: "I wish that every year, at the last ball, the young girl, who during the preceding one has comported herself most decently, most modestly, and has most pleased everyone in the judgment of the members of the box, be honored with a crown . . . which she will bear throughout the year" (130). Rousseau goes to great lengths artificially to exclude rivalry from these primitive beauty contests. Everything that was essentially competitive in the context of the theater ends up being arbitrarily converted in the festival. The lavish expenditures of theater society find their equivalents in all the spending for the contests: "All festivals of this sort are expensive only insofar as one wishes them to be" (127). Feminine rivalry, fanned by the need for adornment and by the exhibition of beauty—the whole world of feminine ostentation fostered by the theater—magically disappears. Is beauty "not a gift of nature just as talents are?"; adornment, "having an innocent and laudable object, would there be entirely in its place" (130, 131). In these festivals, merit and beauty—characterized in the second *Discourse* as the vices of the fledgling society—appear unburdened of their evil content. Let us recall the context of the *Discourse:* "Each one began to look at the others and to want to be looked at himself, and public esteem had a value. The one who sang or danced the best, the handsomest, the strongest, the most adroit or the most eloquent became the most highly regarded. And this was the first step toward inequality and, at the same time, toward vice" (64). Now through public festivals this vice is miraculously restored into virtue; the first evils (vanity and envy) are somehow effaced by civil celebrations. The republic is reconciled with itself in the spectacle of its idealized representation. Man should thereby be prevented from imagining another representation of himself, from envying a better condition. In every aspect of the festival, Rousseau offers models of emulative hierarchy (the army, the family, ranking by age). In *The Government of Poland,* Rousseau's chapter on festivals indicates this distinctive equality: "Let there be frequent open-air spectacles in which different ranks would be carefully distinguished, but in which, as in ancient times, all the people would take equal part."[25]

As Rousseau never tires of explaining, these festivals celebrate social peace; they are demonstrations of universal accord. Their ritual dimension is striking: discipline and hierarchy heed the dictates of rite. Rousseau, however, in a sort of rustic romanticism, seems oblivious to this aspect. Yet all seems to point in this direction. The order and regularity of the festivals, which seem to stifle any spontaneity, appear in the text of the *Letter to M. d'Alembert* as a way of warding off social violence and averting any disintegration through conflict. Thus, rivalrous confrontation may appear, but only in forms that restrict real violence.

Conflict is perfectly ritualized, aestheticized. René Girard underlines the ambivalence of rituals: "Rituals consist in the paradox of transforming the conflictual disintegration of the community into social collaboration."[26]

La nouvelle Héloïse offers a perfect example of the transformative festival: this one takes place during the grape harvest in Valais. Combining work and celebration, harvest time blurs the passage from one activity to the other. The Valais community puts itself on show, effacing hierarchical distinctions in the process. There is a continual reversibility of social orders (Rousseau insists: no exclusion, no preference), with harmony and tranquility. Everything is done to deflect any possible discord. Paradoxically, one of the means for doing so seems to be the simulation of discord. Rousseau writes: "Union itself engenders playful quarrels, and people only irritate each other in order to show how much confidence they have in each other."[27] This statement indicates the fragility of this artificially peaceful community, highlights the fear of violent anarchy, and reveals the community's desire to guarantee its reconciliation. At the end of the episode, the ritual dimension of what Rousseau terms a form of "Saturnalia" is confirmed even more strongly.[28] Once again, festivity absorbs work. Competition reappears but is immediately sublimated:

> When it is nearing quitting time, Madame de Wolmar says: "Let us light the fireworks." Everyone immediately picks up their stack of hemp, honorable sign of their work; they carry it triumphantly to the middle of the courtyard, gather it up into a heap, and make a trophy of it; they set fire to it, but not just anybody has this honor; Julie passes the flame, presenting the torch to the man or woman who has done the most work that evening. . . . The distinguished ceremony is accompanied by cheering and clapping. The hemp burns brightly and clearly, climbing as high as the clouds, truly a bonfire [literally, a fire of joy] around which they skip and laugh. Then everyone is offered something to drink; everybody drinks to the health of the winner.[29]

Celebrating the winner has the power to bring the community together. It could easily be said that in this new solidarity rivalry is sacrificed.[30] Everyone is united around the individual who emerges triumphant from the struggle. There is something of the expiatory in the fireworks; rallying a peaceful crowd around them, the fires partake of the religious in a genuine immolation. The community makes a pact with itself. It sacralizes itself.

In his *Letter to M. d'Alembert*, Rousseau asks these surprising questions about the festival: "What then will be the objects of these entertainments? What will be shown in them? Nothing, if you please" (126). This representational void may well indicate the uniqueness of the festival in that it doubles (and annuls) representation by multiplying mirror effects and by inverting roles between spectators and actors.[31] But from an anthropological perspective, this nothingness can also signify the exclusion of the ancient object of conflict, the suppression of all that may lead to division in society. Nevertheless, in its very absence the object continues to challenge the community; in the end, the participants' gaze focuses on this mysterious place, unoccupied, devoid of any object. The madness of the festival resides precisely in its willful lack of meaning. No longer is there any object: the community is delivered over to itself in the movement of a reconciliation that is not overtly acknowledged but privately experienced.[32]

The Reason of the General Will, the Passion of the Social Contract

The festivals we have just analyzed are the most exalted manifestations of the general will in Rousseau's work. Having thus anticipated my interpretation of the essay *On the Social Contract*, I must now backtrack.

Robert Derathé is among those critics who see the *Social Contract* as an attempt to rehabilitate social man. According to this view, Rousseau distances himself from these ideas in the *Discourse*. Man's isolation must be deemed once and for all a theoretical abstraction, purely hypothetical, which Rousseau supposedly makes use of to develop his system. It is a fiction of bygone days. Derathé cites numerous passages of the text as proof of this change of direction in Rousseau's thought. Isolated man is nothing but a nostalgic flight of fancy. It behooves us, in Derathé's view, to admit that the *Social Contract* was written in the spirit of man's essential desire for reciprocity. In support of this notion, Derathé quotes from the *Fragments politiques*: "It is through reciprocal association that man's most sublime faculties come into being and that the excellence of his nature becomes evident."[33]

I am not entirely convinced that Rousseau's thinking underwent such a marked change; to my mind, the *Social Contract* evinces a solid continuity with his first political writings, while achieving a more incisive analysis of the ambivalence of key concepts in his philosophical system. The miracle of the social contract lies in the balance it achieves between humanity's innate isolation and the artificial reciprocity that results from the pact. Moreover, the system of exchange it involves is quite paradoxical. The theoretical foundation of the general will extends certain concepts found in the *Discourse*, in particular the structure of *amour de soi:*

> The commitments that bind us to the body politic are obligatory only because they are mutual, and their nature is such that in fulfilling them one cannot work for someone else without also working for oneself. Why is the general will always right, and why do all constantly want the happiness of each of them, if not because everyone applies the word *each* to himself and thinks of himself as he votes for all? This proves that the quality of right and the notion of justice it produces are derived from the preference each person gives himself, and thus from the nature of man.[34]

Rousseau reiterates this notion throughout the *Social Contract,* and the passage that defines the general will clarifies the issue definitively: "The act of association includes a reciprocal commitment between the public and private individuals, and . . . each individual, contracting, as it were, with himself, finds himself under a twofold commitment: namely as a member of the sovereign to private individuals and as a member of the state toward the sovereign" (149). The general will functions according to a Leibnizian schema. The monad-individuals communicate with each other through the general will. Louis Althusser was among the first critics to expose the falsity of the contract. He takes this same definition as his point of departure in order to expose Rousseau's sleight-of-hand, or at least his dexterity. Rousseau's contract is indeed a nonexchange. Althusser specifies that "this contract which is not an exchange thus paradoxically has an exchange as its effect. . . . In the Social Contract, man does not give himself completely for nothing. He gets back what he gives and more besides, for the reason that he only gives himself to himself. This must be understood in the strongest sense: he only gives himself to his own liberty."[35] The term *independence* in the *So-*

cial Contract seems to correspond with complete symmetry to the term *isolation* in the second *Discourse*. Taking into consideration the social whole and the relation of its members to the body politic, Rousseau attempts to find the right balance: "This relationship should be as small as possible in regard to the former and as large as possible in regard to the latter, so that each citizen would be perfectly independent of all the others and excessively dependent upon the city" (*Social Contract*, 172).

Let us recall that, in the second *Discourse*, evil issued from the mimetic status of the object as obstacle, in its capacity to attract desire and to incite deadly passions—envy, jealousy, and rivalry—in the hearts of men. Social peace, through the contract, must therefore find a way to efface the object's prestige: it must alienate goods, for this is the only way to extinguish covetousness. In a note that clarifies what Rousseau calls moral equality, acquired thanks to the social pact, he specifies that "it follows that the social state is advantageous to men only insofar as they all have something and none of them has too much" (*Social Contract*, 153). Quite clearly, what Rousseau is attempting to avoid through the contract is the violence of the potlatch, the economic equivalent of the law of talion, according to which each gift calls for an obligatory payback. But the contract becomes a sort of general potlatch: individual wealth is canceled out by a single communal wealth. This also allows Rousseau to sidestep all the traps of gratitude, the rivalry run amok, and the struggles for prestige entailed by potlatch. In *La nouvelle Héloïse*, Clarens is the successful model for this type of alienation: "Nobody envies another's employment; nobody thinks that he may increase his fortune except through the increase of the public wealth."[36]

Rousseau distinguishes in this context between the general will and individual will. Individual will is the reflection of private interest, which in turn has its source in *amour-propre*. Aptly describing the threat that private interest holds for the pact, Althusser writes that "one particular interest can only exist as a function of the other particular interests in rivalry, in universal competition."[37] And for Althusser, opposition is primary; conflict defines particular individuals and their interests. The chapter in the *Social Contract* on suffrage depicts the disorder created by the war of individual interests (bk. 4, chap. 2). The general will seeks harmony and unanimity; it does not tolerate contradiction, turmoil, or dissension.[38] What will make possible this extraordinary transfer of individual wealth to the commonwealth? Humankind's desire for selfish possessions must give way to a desire for love of country: an idealized polarization of desires must take place. Patriotic passion absorbs individual human passions, converting their violent reciprocity into a sole transcendent passion. In Rousseau's system, patriotic love rests on an idealization that directly affects the individual, who seeks his most profound self in heroism and courage. In this sense, love of country is superior to love of humanity, which aspires too abstractly to the universal (through equality and charity).[39] In the last chapter of the *Social Contract*, Rousseau takes up the consideration of a civil religion, the kind of religion most suited to uniting citizens. The notion cannot be a complete success: a civil religion would lead us to theocratic forms entailing serious consequences, such as superstition, religious wars, and tyranny.[40] Rousseau is therefore led to sacralize the social contract itself, to endow it with a transcendence in relation to itself, to exteriorize it as a cult with "the sanctity of the social contract and of the laws. These are the positive dogmas" (226).

The Divine Legislator

The time has come to examine the tremendous role played in the *Social Contract* by the legislator, who is responsible for enlightening the general will. He appears as a physician to society, ready to cure, or warn of, the ills that menace the body politic from within: "The general will is always right, but the judgment that guides it is not always enlightened. . . . The good path it seeks must be pointed out to it. It must be made safe from the seduction of private wills" (162). How, then, shall the citizens be "persuaded," as Rousseau puts it, to the general will (164)? Here, the sacred character of the legislator—his extraterritoriality—becomes apparent: "The legislator is in every respect an extraordinary man in the state." Rousseau emphasizes the radical exclusion of this figure: "It is a particular and superior function having nothing in common with the dominion over men" (163).

It has been observed that Rousseau's own qualities shine through this portrait of the legislator. Jean Starobinski comments on the singular status sought by Rousseau, who refuses to belong to the universal community: "Banished from the community and having severed all immediate bonds to other human beings, he sets himself the task of imagining the bases on which a more just community and a more satisfying form of intimacy could be set up."[41] In *Le parasite,* Michel Serres goes even further in describing the sacred dimension of Rousseau's position: "The author of the *Social Contract* is obviously the superior man, the sage, he who is capable of transforming each person into a part of the great whole. He is beyond passions yet knows them intimately; he is outside the contract, yet foresees it and crafts it. He is unique, he is almost a god, and here he is alone on the earth."[42] Georges Benrekassa sees the legislator—a man of "miracles"—as a limit and a myth that is "indispensable to the formation of the social."[43] In his view, the mythic power of the legislator and his capacity for founding a community stem essentially from his power to overturn human nature.[44]

But we must now ask a fundamental question: what is the source of the legislator's power to bind the community? In other words, what is his specifically religious capacity? Rousseau says once again that he must "have recourse to an authority of a different order"; the legislator's divinity resides in his "great soul" (164, 165). This is what he still retains of the religious and what prevents him from invoking the deity in order to guarantee social peace. Rousseau takes pains to dissociate the divine legitimacy of his legislator from charlatanism, practiced by anyone who "finds [various] crude methods of imposing his beliefs on the people" (165). At this point he seems to be attacking Voltaire, who viewed the religious function of the first legislators as sheer imposture: "And while *amour-propre*-ridden philosophy or the blind spirit of factionalism sees in them nothing but lucky impostures, the true political theoretician admires in their institutions that great and powerful genius which presides over establishments that endure." And Rousseau adds: "We should not, with Warburton, conclude from this that politics and religion have a common object among us, but that in the beginning stages of nations the one serves as an instrument of the other" (165).

What, then, is the legislator's secret? It resides, I believe, in his ability to give an ideal to the community, to make it conform to a common ideal. Thus the good legislator is the one who best knows the mores of a nation, the one who is able to isolate men in their characteristic difference, to enable them to represent themselves as a group. Now we can understand Rousseau's comments on customs and manners. We have already encountered the problem in Montesquieu, to whom Rousseau refers in this context; mores were explained in terms of unanimity, in terms of mimetic fusion.[45] Rousseau takes up the question again in the same way; he makes mores the principle, the law of social organization, "the most important [law] of all":

> It is not engraved on marble or bronze, but in the hearts of citizens. It is the true constitution of the state. Everyday it takes on new forces. When other laws grow old and die away, it revives and replaces them, preserves a people in the spirit of its institution and imperceptibly substitutes the force of habit for that of authority. I am speaking of mores, customs, and especially of opinion, a part of the law unknown to our political theorists but one on which depends the success of all the others; a part with which the great legislator secretly occupies himself, though he seems to confine himself to the particular regulations that are merely the arching of the vault, whereas mores, slower to arise, form in the end its immovable keystone. (172)

Manners are important in Rousseau's mind because they contain the idea of an internal, self-reproducing hierarchical organization. Rousseau situates them between two exteriorities, passions and laws (negative and corrective forces, respectively): "Because customs are the moral standards of the people; and the moment the people cease to respect them, there is no other rule than their passions and no means of curbing them than laws."[46] At this point the legislator's work comes into play. It acts to make an already existing union coalesce, reinforcing it by conferring a concept upon it: "What people, therefore, is suited for legislation? One that [finds] itself bound by some union of origin, interest or convention" (169). But above all, the spirit of the nation must be radically antecedent:

> For an emerging people to be capable of appreciating the sound maxims of politics and to follow the fundamental rules of statecraft, the effect would have to become the cause. The social spirit which ought to be the work of that institution, would have to preside over the

institution itself. And men would be, prior to the advent of laws, what they ought to become by means of laws. (164)

Rousseau takes pleasure in naming his model legislators— Moses, Lycurgus, Numa—of whom he writes in *The Government of Poland:*

> All these legislators of ancient times based their legislation on the same ideas. All three sought ties that would bind the citizens to the fatherland and to one another. All three found what they were look- ing for in distinctive usages, in religious ceremonies that invariably were in essence exclusive and national, in games that brought the citizens together frequently, in exercises that caused them to grow in vigor and strength and developed their amour-propre and self es- teem; and in public spectacles that, by keeping them reminded of their forefathers' deeds . . . stirred their hearts, set them on fire with the spirit of emulation, and tied them tightly to the fatherland— that fatherland on whose behalf they were kept constantly busy.[47]

The case of Moses is exemplary. Rousseau shows how the prophet was able to isolate the Jewish people, to give them an al- most obsessional sense of their autonomy:

> Moses devised for them customs and practices that could not be blended into those of other nations and weighted them down with rites and peculiar ceremonies. He put countless prohibitions upon them, all calculated to keep them constantly on their toes, and to make them, with respect to the rest of mankind, outsiders forever. Each fraternal bond that he established among the individual mem- bers of his republic became a further barrier, separating them from their neighbors and keeping them from becoming one with those neighbors.[48]

The Jewish nation is "utterly faithful to its law" like the Spartans, who under the rule of Lycurgus are passionately patriotic: "He saw to it that the image of the fatherland was constantly before their eyes—in their laws, in their games, in their homes. . . . He saw to it that they never had an instant of free time that they could call their own."[49]

How does the government maintain this coercive patriotism? Beyond emulation of the fatherland itself, it seems that Rousseau has no choice but to go back to rivalry, to create less abstract strategies of emulation, a relation of mediation that requires the human example. Take the case of Poland. Rousseau refuses the notion that this country should rely on the representationality of wealth, on finances, on the newfound transcendence of money: "Money, at best, merely supplements men; and that which supplements is never so valuable as that which is supplemented"; "money . . . is not wealth, but merely an evidence of wealth; and what you must multiply is not the evidence of wealth but rather the thing itself."[50] He even remarks elsewhere that "not only is money a sign, but it is a relative sign that has a true effect only through unequal distribution."[51] If inequality of rank persists in Poland, the rivalries that it provokes do not affect the realm of goods. On the contrary, they encourage positive emulation: "Inequality of rank is offset by the advantage always conferred by a nobility, namely, that the holders of the various ranks are more avid of honors than of gain."[52] The hierarchical apparatus that Rousseau proposes for Poland is based not on wealth but on moral dignity:

> I should like . . . that the rich man who is merely rich shall enjoy neither deference nor approval in his fatherland and shall find himself constantly over-shadowed by poor citizens upon whom titles have been conferred. If the rich man wishes to shine in his fatherland, let him have no choice but to serve it, to be upright for ambition's sake, and to aspire, for all that he is wealthy, to posts that only public approbation can bestow on him and that public blame can take away from him at a moment's notice. That is the way to sap the power of wealth and to produce men whom money cannot buy.[53]

The point, then, is to change the object of desire: "Give us your great deeds in small coins" will be Rousseau's adopted maxim.[54]

He adds that a certain amount of the state's seductiveness depends on the ostentation of the hierarchical apparatus, on the brilliance of the objects held high in public esteem: "Far more than people believe, men's hearts follow their eyes and respond to ceremonial majesty; it surrounds authority with an aura of order and discipline that inspires confidence, and that draws a line between authority and those notions of capriciousness and improvisation that keep company with the idea of arbitrary power."[55] It becomes apparent in this context that Rousseau's preferred form of government is not, curiously enough, that of democracy. Democracy can only exist in theory: "Taking the term in the strict sense, a true democracy has never existed and never will" (*Social*

Contract, 180). Covetousness threatens democratic equilibrium, which requires extreme equality of rank and wealth in order to endure. The best government is therefore an aristocracy. Rousseau reintroduces separation, hierarchy, and difference. In an aristocracy, positive emulation triumphs. The members who make up the aristocratic government are the models for the people. Rousseau effects what might be called a sacred segmentation within the community. Enumerating the qualities possessed by these models, he asserts that "probity, enlightenment, experience, and all the other reasons for public preference and esteem are so many new guarantees of being well governed" (181). Rousseau has found new priests for the nation. The question of inequality seems to be easily resolved. He suggests that "aristocracy requires somewhat fewer virtues . . . such as moderation among the wealthy and contentment among the poor." He even seems willing to admit the soundness of the aristocratic government's elastic play of differences: "For it appears that rigorous equality would be out of place here. It was not observed even in Sparta." Rousseau's political bias is clear: "It is the best and most natural order for the wisest to govern the multitude" (182). This chosen elite can serve to educate the people who will learn that "more important reasons for preference are to be found in a man's merit than in his wealth" (182).

The laws that govern the polis will also follow the path of wisdom. They will attain perfection when they become their own model, when they become "ancient." They will benefit from what Rousseau calls "the prejudice in favor of antiquity," which "each day renders them more venerable" throughout the passage of the years (195). At last they will bear the mark of a sacred will.

In *The Government of Poland*, Rousseau proposes children's games ("recreational" institutions) as a successful model for the social contract.[56] But later he admonishes: "Do not let the students in your school go off by themselves to play, just for the fun of it. They should play together in public, and for some prize to which they all aspire and which arouses in them the spirit of competition and emulation."[57] Here once again we meet up with the atmosphere evoked by the Geneva festivals. This form of competitive fraternity is none other than patriotism, which is the most sought-after spectacle of competition. Rousseau gives this collective imitation a name: patriotic zeal.[58] The fatherland needs these rituals in order to renew and guarantee its foundation.[59] For Rousseau, the nation is forever being born.

Islands and Nations

The time has come to discuss Rousseau's nationalism, as it results from the isolationist logic of his system. Rousseau is one of the few eighteenth-century *philosophes* to oppose the prevailing fashion of cosmopolitanism. Showing himself to be very anti-European, he constantly speaks out against trade, which for thinkers such as Montesquieu and Voltaire represented an alternative to violence among rivalrous groups and wars between states. For Rousseau, the results of commerce are unequivocally harmful. By facilitating too much communication between men, trade eliminates characteristic differences between groups; it effaces the national spirit of peoples. For these reasons Corsica, for which Rousseau established a draft constitution, presents the ideal model for a nation. Its insularity is its salvation: "Every people has or should have a national character, and if it is lacking, the first thing to be done is to supply one. Islanders, above all, who are the least mixed, the least mingled with other peoples, usually have the most marked character."[60] Rousseau reiterates this notion in the section of *Emile* devoted to travel, where a defense of the idea of nation is actually couched in a philosophical and polemical discussion on what appears to be a new fashion in the eighteenth century. (It is no mere coincidence that the voyage theme is developed in juxtaposition to the summary of the *Social Contract*; this proximity lends a degree of political validation to Rousseau's commentary.) In fact, Rousseau's rejection of commercial exchange crops up throughout his work. In the case of Poland, he counsels "scant preoccupation with the outside world, scant concern about trade, as much emphasis as possible on the multiplication of real goods and consumers."[61]

If money is perceived as a social evil, it is insofar as it facilitates exchange. If money as the general equivalent assures "the very mobility of exchange, its flow,"[62] Rousseau takes an opposing stance: "I admit that money makes exchange more convenient, but do better: make exchanges barely necessary; arrange it so that each person is as self-sufficient as possible."[63] In the preface to *Narcisse* he writes even more categorically:

> The crusades, commerce, the discovery of the Indias, navigation, long distance voyages, and even more causes that I am loathe to talk about, have fostered and increased disorder. Everything that facilitates communication between the various nations brings not the virtues of one nation to another, but its crimes, and alters the mores of the other nation which are fitting to its climate and the constitution of its government.[64]

Rousseau's opposition to trade has roots in the archaic structures of exchange. In the genesis of cultures that he establishes in the *Discourse,* Rousseau already sees evil in the passage from "independent trade" to activities requiring division of labor and exchange of skills, such as metallurgy and agriculture.[65] Metallurgy, in particular, comes under attack as an art that imitates natural violence, recalling "some volcano that, in casting forth molten metal, would have given observers the idea of imitating this operation of nature" (*Discourse,* 66). The *Essay on the Origin of Languages* takes up and develops this narrative of beginnings. The violent origins of culture go back much further, to hunting and the domestication of animals. Pastoral life, which made it possible to move beyond the hunting stage, is the true state of nature: "The pastoral art, father of repose and indolence, is the most self-sufficient."[66] The ideal civil state is that in which forms of reciprocity are reduced to a minimum or are virtually nonexistent. In his *Letter to M. d'Alembert,* Rousseau explains that the civil peace enjoyed by the mountain dwellers stems from the families' autonomy from each other and the restriction of their needs to those they can satisfy themselves: "Each joins in himself all the various crafts . . . and makes all his tools himself" (61). In his commentary on the *Social Contract,* Louis Althusser rightly observes that the economic solution to the social contract reiterates propositions found in the *Discourse:* the urban or rural artisanal class is guaranteed economic independence; it makes "free" trade possible.[67]

La nouvelle Héloïse offers us the perfect example of an autarkical economy: "We may avoid transporting our income by making use of it on the spot. Exchange is avoided by consuming it in nature,"[68] so the owners of Clarens inform us. Then there is the delightful episode at Julie's dinner table, when Saint-Preux is fooled by the names of the wines, which seem foreign to him. And yet they come from the region, and his friend confides to him that "from here you can see the vine that produced all these exotic drinks."[69] A capital or large city is the theoretical antithesis of an island: at the confluence of trade routes, it is the ideal locus of exchange, mingling, and undifferentiation. The city has a corrosive effect on people: "The capital breathes forth a constant pestilence which finally saps and destroys the nation."[70] In *Emile* Rousseau goes one step further: "All capitals resemble one another. All peoples are mixed together in them, and all morals are confounded. It is not to capitals that one must go to study nations."[71]

In this light Rousseau's striking description of the Swiss isolated in the hinterlands, buried under winter snows, presents them as the most primitive state at its most glorious:

> Buried in snow for half the year, they were forced to make provision for the winter; sparsely scattered over their rocky land, they cultivated crops with an exertion that toughened them; continuous labor left them no time to become acquainted with the passions; communication was always difficult, and when snow and ice made it altogether impossible, each in his own hut was forced to be sufficient unto himself and his family, which led to crude but happy industry. Each in his own household practised all the necessary arts and crafts; all were masons, carpenters, cabinet-makers, wheelwrights. The rivers and torrents that divided them gave each, by way of compensation, the means of getting along without his neighbours. . . . Thus is that, in the midst of their precipices and valleys, each, living off his land, succeeded in meeting all his needs amply and desired nothing further. Since needs and interests did not conflict, and no one depended on anyone else, their only relations with one another were those of benevolence and friendship.[72]

Rousseau seems torn between the ideal of the peaceful crowd, with its passion for festivals and its lyrical conviviality, and humanity's necessary isolation as the only guarantor of peace and security. Kindness requires independence. Rousseau therefore carries out this artificial separation from the beginning. He delivers the human being from the social entity. In order to have nothing to desire, man must be alone; he must avoid the trap of the other's presence, or else he will become the prisoner of his fellows' passions. The state of nature is the myth of humankind liberated from fatal mimeticism, from the clashing of looks, interests, and desires. When Rousseau makes man into an inexorably social being, he cannot stop himself from conjuring up the nostalgia of man's first solitude. He sets out to describe civil man but, at the same time, irresistibly invents an impossible double: man in the state of nature. Man in the civil state is jealous of his imaginary brother's perfection. Modernity will never allow this hypocritical schism to recede from memory.

Rousseau himself, in his theoretical sacrifice, embodies the complexity, the double impossibility of community life. Jean Starobinski has shown how Rousseau becomes the center, the inventor, and the dispenser of the mental theater that the festival represents. The joy of collectivity lights up his face as if it were his own work.[73] Or else, he is left with the choice of the exile, the foreigner—and yet it is precisely in opposition to the foreigner that Rousseau is moved to create the identity of the people. Faced with the unanimity mustered against him, Rousseau feels as if he has invented the collective, as if he has produced it in spite of himself. He ends up fleeing humankind because he has loved it too much. His final abode is the island of Saint-Pierre—actually separated into two islands, of which he chooses the smaller one. There, he watches nature close in on him: his paradise is also his tomb. In the *Social Contract*, Rousseau alluded to monarchs untouched by historical violence: "We cannot deny that Adam was the sovereign of the world, just as Robinson Crusoe was sovereign of his island, so long as he was its sole inhabitant. And the advantage this empire had was that the monarch, securely on his throne, had no rebellions, wars or conspirators to fear" (143).

In contrast, there is the reverie that Rousseau offers in the Sixth Walk, when he imagines the extraordinary seduction (and no doubt the terror) of absolute power: "If I had been the possessor of the ring of Gyges, it would have freed me from dependence on men and made them dependent on me. In my castles in Spain, I have often asked myself what use I would have made of this ring; for it is surely here that the temptation to abuse would be close to the power to do so."[74] But the phantasm of his natural generosity alone prevails:

Perfectly disinterested with respect to myself and having only my natural inclinations as law, for a few acts of severe justice I would have performed a thousand merciful and equitable ones. Minister of Providence and dispenser of its laws according to my power, I would have performed miracles wiser and more useful than those of the Golden Legend and the tomb of St. Médard.[75]

Nietzsche would have seen this dream as evidence of Rousseau's moral indecency, the moralistic self-seduction of the priest. Rousseau's judicial *jouissance* is the exalted revenge of the pariah who remains a political Narcissus.

This lone monarch, sovereign to his own desire, however, performs the ultimate retreat from history. This is Rousseau's last effort to retrieve the condition of the primitive man and the solitary society of his distant neighbors. The islander is the perfect hero of isolation; he avoids the dangers of exchange and the obligations of reciprocity with others. His solitude is the high price of his newfound autonomy. It is clear now that the small, autarkical societies invented by Rousseau did not go far enough in their effort to meet the demands of the ideal. The solitary walker had to become his own model of a happiness to be found only away from the faces of humanity.

4 / Taking Positions (Diderot)

The Sovereign Mime

Rameau's Nephew, a cynical rewriting of the great political texts of the eighteenth century, deals a deathblow to their prestigious concepts. That it already presents the reverse face of the moral writings of the period should not surprise us. Diderot might well have asserted, along with the Nephew, that "I recall whatever others have said, whatever I have read, and I add to all this my original contribution, which is surprisingly abundant."[1] This said, it remains for us now to prove his claim. We must strip the mores depicted by Diderot's text of their strictly moral component and grant the term *moeurs* the more political sense it took on, in my view, beginning with Montesquieu—a sense relayed by Rousseau as well. In its rigor, *Rameau's Nephew* is a political treatise; it is unquestionably a meticulously carried-out anthropological analysis. The polemical style and artistic dialogue might fool some readers. But its satire, its playful surface, is in fact the aesthetic condensation of a deliberately political reflection.

Diderot, it is true, did not leave behind a great political treatise in the strict sense. There is nothing in his corpus equal to *The Spirit of the Laws* or *The Social Contract*. This omission was actually a calculated move, as Diderot preferred to plunge politics into the vortex of human contradictions. We could say that the very element that constituted the stumbling block to his predecessors' theories—what I have called the obscure realm of morals and manners—became Diderot's preferred object of contemplation for a text like *Rameau's Nephew*. In this context the concept of manners automatically becomes less distinct. Diderot calls manners essentially "variable" (50). We shall see.

In effect, Diderot ended up writing his own *Discourse on the Origins and Foundations of Inequality among Men*. Of all Rousseau's writings, this title appealed to the encyclopedist more than any other, as Rousseau tells us in *The Confessions*. Diderot had previously supplied a few suggestions to Rousseau; it was now time, around 1761, to compose a work of his own. He succeeded brilliantly with *Rameau's Nephew*.

Diderot portrays social man as an imitative being par excellence: this is precisely what the merry-go-round of pantomime is all about. Diderot's text penetrates imitation as an X ray exposes evil, in the sense in which Jacques Derrida uses the term when he identifies the problem in Rousseau: "Evil is a result of a sort of perversion of imitation, of the imitation within imitation." This "corruption of imitation," he continues, is its "monstrous anomaly."[2] Mime is a virtually genetic trait in the Nephew: when nature "slapped together his nephew, she made a face, then another face, and still another" (77). We witness a series of bona fide identity crises in *Rameau's Nephew*. By dint of resembling others, Jean-François Rameau becomes dissimilar to others. Paradoxically, his whole gallery of roles, the carousel of copies, combines to produce his "originality" (9). Diderot says that his character "was getting into a passion" (66); the Nephew becomes an orchestra of voices, personality traits, and emotions, "being in himself dancer and ballerina, singer and prima donna, all of them together and the whole orchestra, the whole theater; then redividing himself into twenty separate roles" (68). The Nephew is a result of these contradictions; he is the twisted figure of these metamorphoses. He therefore changes with his circumstances; he is inconstant, motley, a vacillator through and through. Diderot has created a character of alternation, precariously perched in unstable equilibrium, uneasy and uneven (60).

The mime artist appears as an excessive version of Rousseau's actor, who is in turn the exacerbated figure of civil man. Diderot turns human beings' dependence on others into a parasitical relationship. Going further than Rousseau and, it might be said, pontificating less, Diderot makes a striking declaration of modernity. Rousseau locates the corruption of the civil state in the chiasmus of human needs, which in turn necessitates mutual aid and the sharing of tasks. Diderot does not disagree. He even places humans in a chain of parasitism. He evokes "Nature's table"—"Whom does the savage beg from? The earth, the animals and fishes, the trees and plants and roots and streams" (84)—but only to add immediately that it is "badly served," that it is an "austere diet" (84). In *Rameau's Nephew*, inequalities are orchestrated like some sensationalized ballet. Diderot has chosen to write a "beggar's pantomime" (83). But the state of nature is hardly better in Diderot's view; it even becomes the model for the civil state. Like the latter, the natural relation feeds on parasitism and predation. We must accept this terrible truth: "In Nature all species live off one another; in society all classes do the same" (33). Michel Serres effectively makes the link between parasitology and anthropology. His *Le parasite* is a modern version of Rousseau's second *Discourse*, incorporating the corrective of the informational and biological sciences. The terms of their discussions bear a striking family resemblance: "Mammalian reproduction is an endo-parasitical cycle. We parasite each other to speak, to eat, to organize injustice and legal extortion; for these projects everyone is good."[3] The function of the parasite in *Rameau's Nephew* is to achieve equilibrium in the general circulation of goods. The parasite, too, must host some other parasite; the predatory cycle must be prolonged to the point of saturation. Diderot comes up with a term to describe this phenomenon precisely: the parasite *makes restitution* (33). This is a legal term used in connection with property. Restitution could be seen as an act of revenge carried out on the other's goods. Parasitism consists in squandering the other's wealth. Diderot inaugurates a new conception of political economy, according to which private vices do not, perhaps, lead to the public good, but here and there various intelligent strategies for maintaining general stability are to be found. Parasitism does not lead to an egalitarian system—far from

it. But it does destabilize hierarchies. The chain of dependencies
is contaminated from top to bottom. Parasitism is a new way of
conceiving of exchange. The parasitical relation should be granted
the same conceptual force, for example, as that conferred upon
Adam Smith's invisible hand.

The pantomime-parasite is the sum of all trades and professions.
He or she assumes all positions. A "positional ballet" is a clever
way to describe the interaction of needs in the civil state: it is a
complex choreography of the parasitical intertwining of society.
Diderot found a way of saying, like Rousseau, that man is always
man's man: "Whoever stands in need of another is needy and
takes a position. The King takes a position before his mistress and
before God: he dances his pantomime steps. The minister trips it
too, as courtier, flatterer, footman and beggar before his king. . . .
Really, what you call the beggar's pantomime is what makes the
world go round" (83). In the *Histoire philosophique et politique
des établissemens et du commerce des Européens dans les deux
Indes*, which Diderot revised, the Abbé Raynal describes a stronger
version of this courtly mimeticism. Raynal disparages the prince's
ostentatious display: "The great lord grovels before the prince,
and the people grovel before the great lord."[4]
  Perhaps the *philosophe* would like to exclude himself from this
universal pantomime. But it seems to me that the only individual
who may claim this privilege is the Nephew, the one who manages to play the whole range of social roles. He is simultaneously
excluded and included. He lives parasitically off all relations, in-
terfering with them, theorizing them, exposing them as only he
can. He must be included among those to whom Diderot attributes an exceptional quality, whom he calls eccentrics: "He is like
a grain of yeast that ferments and restores to each of us a part of
his native individuality. He shakes and stirs us up, makes us
praise or blame, smokes out the truth" (10). This position sacralizes him. The Nephew is outside the circuit of exchange, yet at
the same time he stands at the center of its complex crossroads.
In an extraordinary scene, Diderot allows us to see the exceptional nature of the Nephew's situation, which is pushed to a
point of paroxysm. The Nephew's crisis mimics the social crisis.
With everyone bustling around him, his person becomes the

locus of all social contradiction; he plays out all relations in their dizzying reversibility at the price of his own "madness" (67).[5] The clown, located at the center of the community's passions, has become king. His pantomime unfurls and is unleashed in an explosive rush:

> . . . he is a priest, a king, a tyrant; he threatens, commands, rages. Now he is a slave, he obeys. . . .
> All the "woodpushers" in the café had left their chessboards and gathered around us. The windows of the place were occupied from outside by passers-by who had stopped on hearing the commotion. They guffawed fit to crack the ceiling. But he noticed nothing, he kept on. (67)

This is a strange ritual, indeed. The mime must be absent from himself so that others may come to recognize themselves in his performance; he must be alienated from himself in order to take on the qualities of others. In the reversible logic of alternating emotions that he portrays, he becomes a sort of general equivalent. This privilege is vested in him by virtue of his indeterminacy. The Nephew's pantomime is noisy; it produces an impossible din. Michel Serres says that "the parasite is always an exciter."[6] This would explain the enormous brouhaha that he churns up. Serres again: "It is not uninteresting to have a single operator. It warms the room, gives a fever, increases agitation and thermal disorder."[7]

This episode, which must be accorded its full sacrificial dimension, beautifully elucidates the meaning of the chess game that appears in the text's opening tableau. The Nephew is the king of the chessboard. In a scene splendidly contrived by Diderot, we watch the players leave their game precisely at the moment when the Nephew starts his performance, when his crisis is at its apogee. He ends up occupying the place that was actually reserved for him from the beginning; he is moved from the allegorical scene to the real scene. Soon he will take the place of the dead king.[8] The king is the jester. The Nephew even enacts the split of the royal personage into his own jester, his own fool; his pantomime expresses the alternation of the sacrificial roles. The Nephew corresponds in this instance to the trickster in Native American societies, described by René Girard.[9] An enigmatic passage in Diderot's text conveys this mad reversibility, a sort of mysterious twinship: "A real sage would want no fool; hence he who has a fool is no sage; and if no sage, must be a fool. And were he the King himself, he may be his own fool's fool" (50). Stripping the king of his privilege of extraterritoriality, of exclusion from the sphere of men, Diderot says further on that the prince himself also partakes of the great social pantomime: "The King takes a position before his mistress and before God: he dances his pantomime steps" (83). Adopting a decidedly modern perspective, Diderot also makes the king his own fool in order to mask the sovereign's sacredness, to render his function more fragile. But the *philosophe* resacralizes the king by making him undergo a truly victimlike punishment, for which the Nephew serves as emblem.[10] Diderot pours all his talent into this pantomime, depicting it as a virtual immolation of the Nephew, a staged execution. The Nephew entices all the spectators; his pantomime becomes contagious. His ridiculousness takes its entire meaning from this sacred ritual: it performs a cathartic function. The *pharmakos*, here in the guise of a Harlequin, provokes laughter. Diderot even gives us, in the Nephew's physical contortions and grimaces, an aesthetic equivalent, symbolic of the *diasparagmos*. Roused from his crisis, the Nephew is wearied and distraught, "exhausted, worn-out" (70), waiting for "returning strength and wits" (68). He is physically emptied of his many roles, almost as if he had expelled them through his baroque counterfeitings. The community also emerges from this violent spectacle drained, purged of its pleasure, to return to its erstwhile order: "The crowd around us had withdrawn. . . . The chess players had resumed their boards" (70).

The position of the Nephew contrasts with that of the *philosophe*. Yet the latter would like to be the ideal agent of sociability. Seeking exchange with all people, he would be a sort of general equivalent of probity. The *Encyclopédie* defines him thus (under the heading "Philosophe"): "He tries to make himself agreeable to those with whom chance or choice have made him live."[11] His passion is the social relation; the object of his adoration is society. The *philosophe*'s passion for sociability, it might be said, is a reasoned passion; he is both reasonable and right to love his country. He worships society: this is his new religion.

The *philosophe* appears as a supercitizen, of which he constitutes the paragon. His obsession with the idea of the social grants him this privileged position: "He is filled with ideas for the good of civil society; he knows its principles much better than other men." The philosopher can even supply the model for the sovereign and, in fact, the *Encyclopédie* article quotes this passage from the Roman emperor Antonius: "How happy the peoples shall be when kings are philosophers or when philosophers are kings!"[12] All of which amounts to an arrogant and strictly idealized position for the *philosophe*. A citizen above all suspicion and above all other mortals! He is obsessed with the social order; what he lacks is the gift of multiplicity, of social contradiction. He may wish to meditate on reciprocity, but he lacks a practical genius for relations, a real passion for intersubjectivity. The Nephew, I believe, sets a better example of tuning in to the social. He refuses to be an instrument restricted to a single key. As Diderot says, the Nephew is a veritable orchestra.

Rameau's Nephew makes a show of the relations of reciprocity. The text opens with reciprocity—the meaning that must also be assigned to the chess game—and stages the reciprocal struggle, the hostile relation. The philosophical duel between Lui and Moi mimics this relation of exchange. *Rameau's Nephew* appears almost to have been calculated as a catalog or an encyclopedia of human relations invaded by the negative. Of all relations, vengeance in particular predominates. Once again, the philosophical foretext for *Rameau's Nephew* can be found in Rousseau's second *Discourse*. For Rousseau, paradoxically, the appearance of civility, the earliest tendencies toward mutuality, ends in confrontation. The desire for recognition leads to violence. A wrong quickly turns into an outrage "because along with the harm that resulted from the injury, the offended party saw in it contempt for his person, which often was more insufferable than the harm itself. Hence each man punished the contempt shown him in a manner proportionate to the esteem in which he held himself; acts of revenge became terrible, and men became bloodthirsty and cruel."[13] The difference between a wrong and an outrage is that in the latter the object disappears before the person of the adversary. The object is no longer the object of the dispute. The confrontation takes place directly with the other—in person, it might be said. Outrage turns the adversaries into doubles of recognition— or, as Rousseau says, of consideration.

Rameau's Nephew is situated at the crux of these relations. Diderot piles outrage upon outrage. The first is to be found in the gap between the Nephew and the ancestral model. What our first philosophers offered as the social solution par excellence— imitation of the great men or sages of the nation—seems unattainable here for two reasons: the first is the model itself, which having degenerated is no longer worthy of this status; the second obeys a biological imperative. There is a radical rupture separating the generations; it is not clear that there is communication from one group to the other, that there is any possibility of transfer. Certain genes are not reproduced in the genealogical pattern. Likeness is compromised (72): "A fiber . . . has not been granted me. My fiber is loose, one can pluck it forever without its yielding a note" (71).

In *Rameau's Nephew* the mimetic principle of admiration is affected at its very source. In any case, admiration "is no fun" (38). Great men might be majestic trunks that reach all the way to the sky (16), but virtue is rare in them. All the categories that justify imitation of great men are stripped of their prestige here. They ring hollow: "Virtue is praised but hated. People run away from it, for it is ice-cold"; "virtue earns respect and respect is inconvenient" (38). Great men are not necessarily good, and nature lacks the gift of wisdom—it seems defective on this point. This is not enough to stop the Nephew from being envious, though; rather, he is ruled by this feeling: the passion of envy sums up his behavior. "I am full of envy" (17), he frankly confesses. The model may have fallen from the skies; it deserves neither consideration nor admiration. Nevertheless, the ambivalence of imitation persists in its negative mode:

> All I know is that I'd be quite well pleased to be somebody else, on the chance of being a genius, a great man. I have to admit it. Something tells me I'd like it. I have never heard any genius praised without its making me secretly furious. . . . When I hear something discreditable about their private lives, I listen with pleasure: *it brings me closer to them;* makes me bear my mediocrity more easily. (17; emphasis added)

Envy here already approaches what Nietzsche was later to call *ressentiment* (a word that originally belonged to the lexicon of mechanics, signifying "reaction"). The ego-ideal no longer receives values of excellence exclusively: it is contaminated by the subject's negativity. The model displays all the qualities of an omnipotent rival. Identification takes place, but it is attended by more destructive motivations. The model is affected by the subject's abjection. Diderot says that they become closer; they become doubles, imperfectly mirroring each other. Let us consider this physiognomic detail: "That spinal expression of admiration I mentioned to you. I consider it mine, though the jealous might dispute it. I concede that it had been used before me, but no one had discovered how convenient it is for laughing the while at the coxcomb one is admiring" (44).

The modernity of *Rameau's Nephew* (and Diderot's modernity in relation to Montesquieu and Rousseau) lies in this weakening of the ancestral model, in the rivalrous reciprocity between the model and the obstacle. What comes to light in this text is the end of obligation, the end of all debt owed to the parental model—the original debt of which Nietzsche speaks in *On the Genealogy of Morals,* and which is sanctioned by the successes and sacrifices of the present generation vis-à-vis the preceding one. *Rameau's Nephew* is the filial revolution: its title is well chosen. Consistent with this revolution is the ironic attack against nobility as a perpetuation of original and ancestral qualities: "Talent isn't like noble blood which is transmitted and grows in luster by being handed down from grandfather to great grandson without the ancestor's forcing any abilities on the descendant" (79).

This overthrow of the parental hierarchy also accounts for the Sophoclean allusion: "If your little savage were left to himself and to his native blindness, he would in time join the infant's reasoning to the grown man's passions—he would strangle his father and sleep with his mother" (76).[14] In an acute interpretation of the Oedipus complex, René Girard's *Violence and the Sacred* shows how the conceptual invention of the complex forces us to consider the precedence of the mimetic relation that pits father and son against each other: "A theoretical concept such as the Oedipus complex can only be applied to a society in which reciprocal mimesis has already been established and the model-obstacle mechanism set in motion."[15] In other words, the Oedipus complex is irrefragably modern. It belongs to the age of *ressentiment*. Girard continues: "In order for the double bind to operate, [the father] had also to become the obstacle."[16] In fact, to pursue Girard's commentary further, one might say that in *Rameau's Nephew* Diderot generalizes agonistic mimesis by making the uncle (to which, curiously, he gives priority in the text) and the father into equivalents or similar models; he joins them together into a single cultural model. The splitting of the ancestral figure in Diderot's text allows him to immerse the Nephew in his obsessive envy of genius, to bring his character continually closer to triumphant models of the ego, and to keep him in the twisted abyss of *ressentiment*.

The situations of reversibility between model and rival make their way into the dialogue. Although they are located at different sites, and despite their differences and the moral opposition that defines them, the philosopher is affected by the Nephew. The philosopher's speech betrays his loss of footing; he fails in his persuasive task; losing some of his unity of character, he is prey to conflict. The truth that he vaunts as the univocal expression of his conscience is threatened at times by the glitter of falsehood, by the seductive whirl of perversity: "Did I admire? Yes, I did admire. Was I moved to pity? I was moved. But a streak of derision was interwoven with these feelings and denatured them" (67).

Naturally, the eulogy, as a hymn to the great man, as speech addressed to the ideal-other, becomes a parody in *Rameau's Nephew*. Here is the glorious pantomime of praise the Nephew addresses to himself:

> "Thus you would be told at breakfast that you are a great man, you would read in *Three Centuries of French Literature* that you are a great man, by nightfall . . . that great man, Rameau the Nephew, would fall asleep to the soft hum of praise buzzing in his ears. . . . he would snore like a great man."
> In saying this, he . . . closed his eyes and imitated the blissful sleep he was imagining. (18)

In Diderot's world, admiration becomes yet another position in the ballet of masks.

There is an even more extreme attack on the ideality of admiration that is directed toward another object of desire: money. If there is a model to be venerated, money certainly fills the bill:

> Gold, gold is everything; and everything, without gold, is nothing. Therefore . . . whenever I have a gold piece—not often, to be sure: I plant myself in front of [my son], draw the piece from my pocket, show it to him with admiring looks, raise my eyes to heaven, kiss the gold in front of him, and to show him still more forcibly the importance of the sacred coin, I stammer out the names . . . of all the things one can buy with it. (73)

The very object that Rousseau identified as a force of compromise in relations of exchange is here venerated: money is a mimetic object par excellence, the source of all evils and the motor behind all vices. The gold sovereign has become the monarch that rules the world, the tyrant of human needs. It could even be said that the Nephew occupies the very place of gold; "penetrated by the value of the gold coin,"[17] he is at the center of the circuit of exchange, at the intersection of the circulation of goods. He becomes the gold that fascinates him and that he desires. He is this general equivalent.

Parasitism in *Rameau's Nephew* is the economic equivalent of envy. The *philosophe* seems to escape it, but his Catonism is full of *ressentiment*. He is continually gazing at those higher than himself. He despises the rich, but his "modesty is the prop of pride" (34). In the society described by Diderot, emulation veers toward the negative: what is played out on the social chessboards is the violence of hierarchical relations. Reciprocity has become impossible because the other appears as the enemy at every turn. The bitterness of the social struggle in *Rameau's Nephew* expresses the crisis that affects the community. The text makes a show of various professions ("carpenters, builders, roofers, dancers, and singers" [82]) in order to revoke the idea of these illegitimate classifications. The Nephew is fed up with this "hell of an economy" (82). Nevertheless, the economic crisis is a condensed form of a more general crisis that affects all institutions and the culture as a whole (ancestor worship, weakening of the paternal and royal figures). The ballet of positions, the pantomimes, act out all these reversals: "Each sees in the other the usurper of a legitimacy that he thinks he is defending but that he is in fact undermining."[18]

The various reversals in Diderot's text can also be chalked up to this crisis. *Rameau's Nephew* refuses to be played in a single key. In its perpetual dissonance, it tends toward undifferentiation; Diderot has a fine time producing the rhetorical processes of alternation. Laughter is the end point of the generalized process of desymbolization,[19] which consists of cramming the text with as many contradictions as possible and expunging from it all hierarchical devices. Diderot was right to call his work a satire—a term derived from *satura*, which designates multiplicity, the notion of heterogeneous mixture.[20] It has been observed that the Nephew is a brilliant figure of the Latin concept of *inaequalitas*.[21] The prologue of Diderot's text is placed under the sign of Vertumnus, god of changing seasons and the vicissitudes of weather. The narrator takes us to the Palais-Royal, "place of ill repute for all exchanges and meetings, for conversation, prostitution and gaming."[22] The text repudiates stability, expelling it at every turn. "Saturated" with circumstances, *Rameau's Nephew* is given over to the vacillation of opposites.

General Hostility

The world of the Nephew, a world delivered up to vengeful fury, takes us back to a time before the justice of laws. In this text, the law itself loses its privileged status and takes on the passivity of theory; it is not aligned with natural force. In Diderot's world, the cruel reflex of natural vengeance is more likely to intervene than justice: "We square things up with one another *without benefit of the law*. La Deschamps some time since, and now la Guimard, avenges the King upon his tax collector; after which the dressmaker, the jeweler, the upholsterer, the lacemaker, the confidence man, the lady's maid, the cook, and the saddler avenge the tax collector upon la Deschamps" (33; emphasis added). The universe of *Rameau's Nephew* is entirely overrun by reprisals. Exchanges are characterized by the countergift, an index of malevolent dissymmetry. The Nephew describes a strange contract that perhaps sums up the nature of social relations: "There's a tacit agreement that we'll reap benefits and return evil for good, sooner or later" (55). The countergift loses all its positive value here. Rather than participating in the symmetry of exchange—good for good, gift for gift—the countergift is merely a hostile reply that, in its negativity, nullifies the original intention of the first gift. *Rameau's Nephew* is a world of poisoned gifts.[23] Justice in relations seems to be increasingly absent from the world. Or, rather, in laughter it finds its most untroubled form: "They say, when one thief robs another the Devil laughs" (33).

The Nephew would like to acknowledge a global conscience, a sort of universality or ethical transcendence, but such a possibility is quickly refuted by what he calls *trade idioms*. These idioms rule the world and can, on occasion, multiply to the point of suffocating the universal conscience: "The worse the times become, the more the idioms multiply" (32). In times of crisis, the divisiveness of individual interests intensifies to an extreme, eventually driving out the common conscience. Benevolent reciprocity gives way to exchanges in which selfish competition becomes visible and private interests triumph.

Diderot transforms the human community into a bestiary of wolves, tigers, and panthers. His text, as we know, scores a successful attack on his detractors, but the dance of proper names in the text is beside the point. What is inscribed in the torrential litany of names is pure, expansive reciprocity. Vengeful contagion has turned everyone into doubles; in the end, wrongs and outrages are detached from their origin—they can no longer be traced to a particular source. Hence the symmetry of Diderot's text: "Le Brun cries out that Palissot . . . has made a squib about him. . . . Poinsinet cries out that Palissot has attributed the squib to him. Palissot had to make the attribution and Poinsinet is in the wrong. The little Abbé Rey cries out. . . . the bookseller David cries out. . . . Helvetius may well cry out" (55–56).

The Nephew's final words express precisely this sentiment: he laughs best who laughs last (87). Spiteful reciprocity and combative contagion can be heard in the mimesis of laughter, and this ultimate judgment voices the implacable, inexorably resurgent threat of vengeance. There will always be one more last laugh at the end of the chain. The undifferentiated echo of laughter forces the participants into the repetition of sameness, condemning them to eternal hostility. The bearing of grudges betrays the inability to forget, fixing indelibly the memory of the other as offender. It turns vengeance into a phantasmic desire doomed to remain unfulfilled.

Rameau's Nephew is the fictional precipitate of the polemical condensation linked to the *Encyclopédie*. No longer should the famous dictionary be viewed as a monument to the glory of the *philosophes*, the triumph of a community that has found peace but, rather, as the miracle of a society that was able to steer clear of fatal dissension. Diderot retaliates in some sense for having functioned as the mediator of disagreements. The text of *Rameau's Nephew* is a way of evacuating all the negativity that could have impeded the encyclopedia enterprise. Diderot's text mentions the names of the encyclopedists (Georges-Louis Leclerc Buffon, Montesquieu, Claude Arien Helvétius, d'Alembert, Voltaire) not to come to their defense; in the satire, these proper names introduce a risky ambivalence. What is more, Diderot expresses himself using the terms of his own detractors. He imports their ideas into his own text, and this juxtaposition results in an ambiguous contiguity. We can never know who is speaking in this text, Diderot or his opponents: "We'll prove that Voltaire has no genius; that Buffon is always on stilts like the turgid declaimer he is; that Montesquieu was only a wit. We'll tell D'Alembert to stick to his ciphering" (34). Satire devours everything, throwing all meanings into confusion.[24] When Diderot writes the article "Encyclopédie" aiming to take stock of his work and record his last wishes in regard to this monstrous object, he refers to the harmful force of *"esprit de corps,* which is ordinarily petty, jealous, concentrated" and which by stifling the voices of multiplicity or variety is capable of destroying all projects of this kind.[25] Diderot describes a utopian community of scholars as *"men bound together by the common interests of the human race and by a feeling of mutual good will,"* yet he saddles these same men with a censor, whose role is to facilitate the exchange of differences.[26] As we know, Diderot will assume this role to the point of exhaustion.

Rameau's Nephew reveals to us a world from which all kindness has taken leave. Goodwill is relegated to a long-ago era, to time immemorial. It is a nostalgic emblem. Ancient hospitality has been transformed into universal hostility. The meals at Bertin's and Choiseul's that frame the satire are positive proof of this change. Gift-giving has been replaced by slander; unmotivated generosity has given way to self-interest. In his *Observations sur le Nakaz*, which Diderot wrote for the benefit of Catherine II, Diderot's definition of society makes no bones about these conflicts: "The word *society* makes one think of a state of union, of peace, of the concourse of all individual wills toward a common goal, the happiness of all. The reality is the exact opposite. Society is a state of war; war of the sovereign against his subjects; war of the subjects amongst themselves."[27] This diagnosis finds its illustration in *Rameau's Nephew*, a text in which music appears as a tumultuous, dissonant symphony. Diderot exploits this political metaphor to its utmost (it had already appeared in Montesquieu and it is also found in Rousseau). Pantomime is even better—a brouhaha, an unchecked hullabaloo that is Diderot's way of expressing every one of the passions. Music must embody multiplicity; it must be polyphonous.[28]

The civil state is a state of war. In his political writings, Diderot uses mechanical metaphors in order to express social conflicts. We find the following remarkable description in *Entretiens avec Catherine II*:

> In the so-called state of simple nature, men were scattered over the surface of the earth like an infinity of little springs, each in isolation. From time to time some of these little springs would meet, press too tightly against each other, and break. The legislators, witnessing these accidents, sought a remedy, and what did they come up with? Their idea was to bring these little springs together and put them into a fine machine, which they called society; and in this fine social machine, the little springs, animated by an infinity of differing and opposing interests, acted and reacted against each other with all their strength, so that any passing instance of accidental war resulted in a state of perpetual war in which all the little springs, weakened and exhausted, were in a constant state of alarm, and more were broken in one year than would have been broken in ten years in the primitive, isolated state in which the only law was the resentment provoked by the shock of impact.
>
> But far worse things were to come. These fine machines called societies multiplied and were squeezed together, so that the impact involved not merely a single spring coming up against another, but one, two, or three of these fine machines clashing against each other. And in this horrific collision, more springs have been broken in a single day than would have been broken in a thousand years of the state of wild and isolated nature.[29]

Diderot does not shrink from the conflict-ridden nature of the social state. He always chooses complexity, the pluralistic expression of passions and interests. Refusing to imagine a social ideality, he conceives society in terms of reciprocity; this, however, is often rife with conflict. Diderot's political pluralism seems to find its strongest support in his materialism. The alternative for him is an escape into metaphysics or geometry. Jacques Chouillet was right to emphasize that these metaphors are not mechanical in the traditional sense of the word but, rather, organicist.[30] The political machine cannot be understood without fully taking into account "friction," "collisions," and "resentments." Diderot belongs wholly to the liberal tradition. Politically, he is not far from the Montesquieu who praises England for giving free rein to all its passions. What Diderot as well finds interesting in the organization of English society is the play of forces that counterbalance the sovereign's powers, the division of powers in the state. To counteract the temptation of despotism, Diderot proposes the virtue of political counterforces: "Objections raised regarding the physical counterforces of a political body, which keeps the sovereign authority under surveillance, do not seem well founded to me, as proved by the English Parliament, which appears as a formidable counterforce to the king's power."[31] In contrast to Rousseau, who, faced with the inevitability of conflict, offered man the shelter of his original solitude, Diderot makes a case for the gregarious imperative: "Isolated man had only one adversary, nature. Man united has two, man and nature. United man therefore has a more urgent motive to close ranks."[32] He will reiterate this idea: "In any society of men, the more scattered the parties are, the less they band together; the further this society strays from the true notion of society, the less they support each other; the less they help each other out, the weaker the society."[33] Diderot avoids singling out individuals, preferring rather to think of men united in bands, massed in a crowd: "Take a look at this crowd [of characters] in the moment of agitation: each individual's energy is exerted in all its violence; and because not one is endowed with precisely the same degree of energy as another . . . there is not one who is equal in action and position [to any other]."[34] Diderot also uses the expression *reciprocal action* to describe group mimetic effects. Jean Starobinski points out that the expression is an abbreviated form of action and reaction, and he recognized that it, too, involves "phenomena of crowd formation."[35] In his examination of government crises, Diderot considers relations of emulation and rivalry, which he sees provoking the collapse of hierarchical structures:

> The democractic state might be represented by a great multitude of balls, more or less equal, placed on one plane and pressing against each other; the level remains the same, but the pressure varies according to the mass of the balls. In a monarchical state, the balls form a pyramid. . . .
> When the balls are arranged horizontally, the jolts work their way from side to side. When they are in a pyramid, the jolts are transmitted from the bottom up. In a democratic state, everyone wants to have elbowroom; in a monarchy everyone wants to attain the level above his own. In the first state, emulation seeks to take up space; in the second it means to climb higher.[36]

The political map of the world that Diderot establishes is the polar opposite of the one Rousseau creates: travel, commerce, capitals setting up trade relations with towns and villages. This turbulent, multifarious circulation generates an accelerated, arborescent growth of exchange networks. There is thus a shift "from the state of hamlets to the state of villages, from the state of villages to the state of market towns, and from these to the state of small, medium-sized, and then big towns and cities."[37] What interests Diderot in each case are the relations. Starting with the simplest interaction, Diderot goes to the most complicated organizations, always foregrounding the necessity for reciprocity. Not by chance does the *Observations sur le Nakaz* sing the praises of citizens who are shopkeepers or merchants, whose role in the state is almost as important as that of the sovereign. An essentially cosmopolitan person himself, Diderot understands the trader's necessary connective function: "He belongs to all nations; so much the better; all nations therefore have an equal interest in protecting him; he discriminates against no one, whether he buys or sells; so much the better; partiality would restrict his circumstances."[38]

Hospitality

If we set out to paint a picture of Diderot's anthropological thought, we are obliged to turn to the *Supplement to Bougainville's "Voy-*

age." It does indeed take up the debate concerning the state of nature and the civil state, but in fact it should be read as a supplement to the *Discourse on the Origin and Foundations of Inequality*. Diderot composes his own politics of travel, problematizing the issue in a very sophisticated manner. The *Supplement* responds to those who disparage Diderot's cosmopolitanism, such as Palissot and Fougeret de Monbron: if *Rameau's Nephew* represents a polemical stage, this will be followed by a theoretical reaction in the form of the *Supplement*. When in a note to his second *Discourse* Rousseau faults travel accounts he has read on account of their ethnocentrism ("everybody does hardly anything under the pompous name of 'the study of man' except study the men of his country"[39]), he appeals to the wisdom of the *philosophes*—Montesquieu, Buffon, d'Alembert, and Diderot—for reparation. Diderot demonstrates that Rousseau's confidence in him is not misplaced. Bougainville is described as the philosopher-traveler. He "possessed the necessary scientific preparation and he had the requisite personal qualities—a philosophic attitude, courage and veracity . . . and a real desire to see, to learn and to enlighten himself."[40] The traveler must renounce the reassurance of his customary foundations because he is pledged to the inconstancy of the waters and the diversity of peoples. Diderot's text offers proof of a degree of withdrawal from ethnocentrism; he accomplishes this, paradoxically, by universalizing what is relative:

> This account of Bougainville of his voyage is the only book that has ever made me hanker after another country than my own. Up to now, I had always thought that a person was never so well off as when at home. Consequently I thought that everyone in the world must feel the same. All this is a natural result of the attraction of the soil, and this is an attraction that is bound up with all the comforts one enjoys at home and is not so sure of finding away from it. (185)

Rousseau, observing the unsettling effects of distant voyages, originally thought that such effects could be attributed to the national extension of *amour de soi* but in the end rejected this as being insufficient to justify man's attachment to his native land: "What one loves about one's country, what one rightly calls the fatherland . . . is not simply a matter of place, nor simply a matter of things. The object of this love is much closer to us."[41] Rousseau eventually diagnoses the destabilizing effects of travel as stemming from the citizen's intimate connection with the institutions of his country—its laws, morals, and customs. In this sense, Aotourou, who makes the return voyage with Bougainville from Tahiti to Europe, is a bad traveler. Limiting himself to the projection of what is identical, he is closed to all forms of alterity, caught up in the closure of his own language: "He soon got bored, though, living among us. . . . he was never able to learn to speak our language. . . . He grew more and more disconsolate from a desire to be back in his own country" (185).

It is not difficult to understand how the incommunicability of cultures subsequently becomes the main subject of Diderot's book. Indeed, the *Supplement* is a theorization of passage from one place to another and of the possibilities for all forms of exchange. Hence Diderot's fright when confronted with the isolation of Lancer's Island and the anthropological oddity of its inhabitants' customs: "What means of communication were there between them and the rest of mankind?" asks the *philosophe* uneasily (182). If natural accidents can turn the world into an aggregate of isolated spaces, how, then, can any continuity be found? Are we condemned to the impossibility of exchange, to the untranslatability of mores and languages? How are we to bridge these "stretches of impassable sea" that separate cultures (182)? Do we have eyes only to see no farther than ourselves, bounded as we are by our cultural narcissism?

Let us delve further into Diderot's text. Certainly the old man, whose farewell constitutes the second part of the *Supplement*, pointedly addresses his speech to his own native land of Tahiti. Diderot places him in front of a silent Bougainville, who is stupefied by the accusation of colonialism that is hurled at him. Their conversation is a *dialogue de sourds*, with the Tahitian's voice filling up space. I believe that Diderot uses the harangue as a device to accentuate the extremism of the old man's position. He is described from the beginning as having an attitude of indifference, of closure toward the other:

> At the time of the Europeans' arrival, he cast upon them a look that was filled with scorn, though it revealed no surprise, no alarm and no curiosity. They approached him; he turned his back on them and retired into his hut. His thoughts were only too well revealed by his

silence and his air of concern, for in the privacy of his thoughts
he groaned inwardly over the happy days of his people, now gone
forever. (187)

He differs from the other inhabitants in his aggressive xenopho-
bia: "At the moment of Bougainville's departure, when all the
natives ran swarming onto the beach, tugging at his clothing and
throwing their arms around his companions and weeping, the old
man stepped forward and solemnly spoke" (187). His speech must
be read closely in order to sound the depths of his unwavering
rejection of the foreigner. The old man is undoubtedly voicing a
legitimate reaction when he accuses the European of having introduced the notion of property ownership into a community in
which the circulation of goods was previously subject to no codi-
fication. But his recognition of the European is granted only on
the basis of a projection of himself onto the other; respect for the
other takes place only through an identification with the self. A
sort of primary narcissism guarantees an opening toward the other:
"We respected *our own image* in you" (188; emphasis added).

As Diderot chooses to express the old man's speech in specular
terms, these must be given due attention. The European is ac-
cused of being a poisoner: "You have infected our blood," the old
man cries out (189). In rejecting the European for having awak-
ened the sense of alterity in the Tahitian people, the old man refuses the most extreme form of the other's presence. Relations
with others are experienced as a sort of impurity. Hence the expression of nostalgia for a community that is closed in on itself,
left to its perpetual peace, to the lone echo of its flutes and the
wild abandon of its innocent dances.

Nevertheless, a will to power breaks through the old man's
harangue. When he addresses his people in an attempt to repos-
sess them, one might even wonder whether he is not really jealous of Bougainville, who has succeeded in seducing the Tahitians.
Bougainville and the old man are placed in symmetrical positions. They stand facing each other as the emblematic signs of
two irreconcilable cultures. The old man responds to the Europeans' colonial violence with the violence of his own strength
and of the natural superiority of his race: "Take this bow in your
hands—it is my own—and call one, two, three, four of your com-

rades to help you try to bend it. *I can bend it myself"* (189, emphasis added). His suit is successful: at the end of this impassioned speech, the Tahitians all repair to their huts, turning their backs on the Europeans. The sole accompaniment to the departure of Bougainville's companions is silence, a silence that also calls forth the old man's original disdain and overtakes the entire Tahitian community, cloaking the island in its primeval layers: "Nothing was to be heard but the dry whistling of the wind and the dull pounding of the waves along the whole length of the coast" (192). The old man founds the collectivity by holding out to it the possibility of representing itself conceptually as a group. He becomes its leader. This foundation takes place at the cost of an extradition, that of Bougainville who is expelled as other. The Tahitian group is founded against him; its birth is registered as an act of opposition.

The old man's fiery monologue in front of Bougainville can be contrasted with the dialogue between l'Aumônier and Orou. At the outset, each of the two speakers in the dialogue seems to maintain his own position: l'Aumônier speaks in the name of Europe and its culture, Orou speaks in the name of Tahitian society, which is natural society. But Orou favors a mixture that stands in contrast to the old man's rejection of the foreigner. Orou goes as far as to offer his wives to the European traveler. L'Aumônier eventually reconsiders his refusal to share Tahitian customs and ends up integrating himself into Orou's little nucleus. His role is well chosen. Although l'Aumônier stands for those characters who export their beliefs without worrying about the difference of the other, too "taken up by the sublime vocation that calls them," to borrow Rousseau's words,[42] he nevertheless evolves— to the point where his own cultural positions, which appeared rigid at the start of the dialogue, end up losing their solidity.

In the end, the utility and fecundity of the Tahitian nation will be able to benefit from the European presence. The mixture contemplated by Orou will make it possible to share mutual and distinctive qualities; it will soften the hard contours of their singularities. This potential is a far cry from the epidemic feared by the old man. On the contrary, Orou sees the mingling of bloods through miscegenation as the source of profits and advantages for the Tahitian nation:

> When you go away, you will leave with us a brood of children. Do you think we could have extracted a more valuable tribute from you than this tax collected from your own bodies and from your own substance? . . . We have vast areas of land yet to be put under the plow; we need workers, and we have tried to get you to give them to us. We have epidemics from time to time, and these losses must be made up; we have sought your aid to fill up the gaps in our population. We have external enemies to deal with, and for this we need soldiers, so we have allowed you to give them to us. We have a surplus of women and girls over men, and we have enlisted your services to help us out. Among these women and girls there are some with whom our men have thus far been unable to beget any children, and these were the ones we first assigned to receive your embraces. . . . We have taken from you and your fellows the only thing we could get from you. Just because we are savages, don't think we are incapable of calculating where our best advantage lies. (211–12)

If one of the fundamental issues in the *Supplement* is the natural circulation of beings within society ("we have developed a kind of circulation of men, women and children" [207]), it can be said without hesitation that a similar circulation is desired between cultures. A unifying thread in Diderot's thought, expressed best in *D'Alembert's Dream*, is the prevailing principle that "all beings participate in the existence of all other beings."[43] In contrast, Rousseau expels the foreigner in order to keep the races pure. For Rousseau, national identity inevitably rears its head. Thus he writes this intentionally shocking sentence in *Emile:* "Every patriot is harsh to foreigners: they are only men; they are nothing in his eyes."[44]

In the *Supplement*, several voyages take place from Europe to Tahiti and vice versa. Some of them, in this spirit of general circulation, are successful (such as l'Aumônier's), while others are failures (those of Aotourou and Bougainville). What determines their success is the traveler's readiness to adapt to the other and to abandon his prejudices. His Europeanized speech notwithstanding, the old man remains deaf to the language of the Europeans. Aotourou remains enclosed within his culture. Conversely, Orou, despite the reputed complexity of the Tahitian language, is able to act as a translator: "You who understand the speech of these men"

(188). He makes the effort to approach alterity. In Diderot's text, this adaptability goes by the name of politeness: the chaplain (l'Aumônier) who displays it is called "courteous" (216).

In the conclusion to the *Supplement*, Diderot reaffirms this wish for adaptability, the necessity to demonstrate openness to the mores of the other without, however, giving up one's own: "Put on the costume of the country you visit, but keep the suit of clothes you will need to go home in" (228). This is a difficult compromise. Costumes and customs—the words are essentially equivalent. The question of travel assumes its definitive response: it is not a matter of discovering sameness, of experiencing the ease of the familiar, but rather of keeping one's nostalgia for the other and of displaying a little forgetfulness of self, like l'Aumônier: "The chaplain ends by assuring us that he will never forget the Tahitians, and confesses that he was tempted to throw his vestments into the ship and spend the rest of his days with them. And he fears that he will have more than one occasion to be sorry he didn't" (217).

There is no place in Diderot for Rousseau's retreat from history, none of Rousseau's sacralization of the laws and civil institutions as a way of escaping the violence of the world. Diderot welcomes a turbulent world, rich with differences, where the energy of each individual is taken into account. Preferring the heterogeneity of the social, he admits rivalry and competition as social realities. As for the essence of human nature, Diderot rejects both Hobbes's warrior and Rousseau's peaceful man. He sees the human condition as a complex equilibrium of good and evil, what he calls "the perpetual vicissitude" of human nature.[45] We could say that Diderot invents a joyful anthropology of complexity, an anthropology of action, in which each person insists on going beyond his or her isolated relationship with him- or herself and with nature to encounter the other. Sociability is for Diderot the greatest challenge, but it is also the most surprising reward.

5 / The Politics of Crime[1]
(Sade)

The Marquis de Sade can be understood only if we observe from
the outset that his work maintains a constant polemical relationship with all the philosophical texts of his century: Montesquieu
and Helvétius are explicitly named, but above all there is Rousseau. In fact, Sade seems to have taken pleasure in taking apart
the Genevan's argument point by point. Or alternatively, Rousseau's text could be seen as providing a chaste palimpsest for
Sade's own text. Rousseau is placed at the center of this book because he plays a central role in his century. Both Diderot and Sade
write in opposition to him, and their respective political theories
are rewritings—cynical in the former case and perverse in the
latter—of Rousseau's thought.

Sade's modernity is unmistakable, yet his work belongs to his
own era, and for too long now the tendency has been to read it out
of context, to isolate it as an eccentric aberration. Sade, in fact,
takes the entire eighteenth century within his prodigious grasp
and iconoclastically does violence to—sodomizes, we might say—
all its positive concepts. Reading Sade along with the *philosophes*
of his century is an easy proposition. Inversion is the modus
operandi of the Sadean text, a contrarian exercise par excellence;

it revels in a war of wills, a conceptual orgy. Sade brings a phe-
nomenal amount of philosophical and anthropological literature
into his writing. In this sense, he could not but signal the end of
the Enlightenment: his work is none other than a negative encyclopedia. Sade remains, in spite of himself, the quintessential
philosopher, peerless among the *philosophes*. His libertine heroes
rattle off the names of one *philosophe* after another, taking anar-
chical and often antagonistic samplings from them; like his hero-
ine Juliette, Sade can defend Hobbes and Montesquieu at the same
time. If Sade's text turns everything upside down, if (contrary to
what is generally believed about it) it refuses systematization, it
is because Sade himself is the culmination of the contradictions
of his time.

The Sadean oeuvre is a paean to inequality, a cold and methodi-
cal correction of Rousseau's second *Discourse*. Sade attacks the
principle of natural pity, which is pivotal in Rousseau's thought.
In *Juliette,* Voldomir, the libertine, defines pity as "the dullest,
most stupid, most futile of all the soul's impulsions."[2] In the
Sadean state of nature all men resemble each other, in everything
but their degree of strength. The strong and the weak immediately enter into a relation of comparison, and the weak are placed
in a position of dependence. But in Sade's scheme, comparison does
not have the same effect as it does in Rousseau's. For Rousseau,
pity leads to benevolence. For Sade, identification is contaminated from the outset by negative mechanisms. What constitutes
the problem of identification in Rousseau is brought to the fore-
front by Sade. In Rousseau's *Discourse* pity operates through
mimetic projection: we identify with others' sufferings out of fear
for ourselves. This analogy is what spurs us to be benevolent.

Rousseau did detect, it is true, a certain narcissistic pleasure or
self-satisfaction in this generous sentiment, but Sade will enlarge
greatly on this tendency. Comparison to someone else's disadvan-
tage becomes pure *jouissance* inasmuch as it is an affirmation of
inequality.[3] Sade lays odds on the egotistic element in pity: "Seeing others beset by woe, we pity them because we fear lest that
same woe befall us" (281). Still further, Sade takes the imperfec-
tion of pity to its most extreme signification. The pathetic scene
betrays a fundamental imbalance—between the unhappy and the
happy, between the strong and the weak. Pity attempts to rectify

a natural evil, to correct a deficiency. In a word, it tries artificially to erase a difference. Pity does indeed equalize: it "becomes a real vice once it leads us to meddle with an inequality prescribed by Nature's laws" (177). Pity is thus a vice in that it strips man of one of his natural attributes.

Rousseau's spectator identified with the other's misfortune through projection, which entailed commiseration. The Sadean spectator, on the other hand, must distance him- or herself from the object of the spectacle and must transform pity into lust.[4] What is required is nonidentification. Or, rather, the mechanism of identification must produce its opposite: one's own happiness must be projected in the face of the other, must be phantasized when one is confronted with the need for pity. The Sadean individual must be able to find *jouissance* in the very contrast. Noirceuil, the libertine, offers an analysis of the problem:

> It is a thousand times sweeter to say to oneself, casting an eye upon unhappy souls, *I am not such as they, and therefore I am their better*, than merely to say, *Joy is unto me, but my joy is mine amidst people who are just as happy as I.* It is others' hardships which cause us to experience our enjoyments to the full; surrounded by persons whose happiness is equal to ours, we would never know contentment or ease: that is why they say, and very wisely indeed, that, to be happy, you ought never look upward, but always at those who are below you. (1161)

One must even, if necessary, create artificial cases of inequality, forcing the other into weakness, making him or her into an object of comparison, in order, in the end, to deny this object any pity: Noirceuil tells Juliette that her "complete pleasure" would consist in "drawing the spectacle of misery into [her] immediate vicinity." His instruction to her: "Improve your enjoyment through comparison as intimate and at the same time as advantageous to you as possible, since all the woe confronting you is of your unique fabrication" (1161–62). Sade telescopes the phases of what appeared in Rousseau as a progression toward inequality. Sadean disequilibrium affects the establishment of law and property, of the magistracy and arbitrary power, and of the different states that result from these: the divisions between rich and poor, powerful and weak, master and slave. The Sadean despot enjoys the advantage in each of these distinctions.

Pity, for Sade, is a sentiment restricted to the weak, who are forced into comparison by the natural inequality of allotments. Hardship being somehow consubstantial with their being, they are steeped in analogies of an unhappy bent. Comparison has quite the opposite function for the strong, whose ascendancy, narcissism, and automony of happiness are thus reinforced. Money operates to the same effect in the mechanism of comparison. As Barthes has pointed out: "Money proves vice and supports bliss: . . . it guarantees the spectacle of poverty; . . . wealth is necessary because it makes a spectacle of misfortune."[5] Veblen has sometimes been alluded to in connection with this Sadean *jouissance* through comparison.[6] The term he uses is *invidious comparison*, with an allusion to the envy and rivalry provoked by comparison. Through such comparison, whoever possesses the object is granted an unattainable position of superiority. Moreover, comparison separates: it excludes the envious from the closed, self-sufficient relation that the possessor maintains with the object. Under the gaze of the envious, the dignity of the object is made equal to the dignity of the possessor. Suddenly, he who has, has all.

Sade's entire corpus could be derived from a principle in Rousseau's that establishes a natural, benevolent reciprocity: "Do what is good for you with as little harm as possible to others."[7] Sade might well have inverted this proposition to enjoin: "Do what is good (or bad) for you with as much harm as possible to others." The same applies to the famous equation that governs erotic reciprocity in Sade, expressed as follows in *Juliette:* "Pray avail me that part of your body which is capable of giving me a moment's satisfaction, and, if you are so inclined, amuse yourself with whatever part of mine may be agreeable to you" (63–64). This proposition should be accompanied by another that recurs like a philosopheme in Sade's writings: man must obtain his happiness "no matter at whose expense" (99).

What has been shattered by Sade is this very principle of benevolence, the same ideal of reciprocity that other *philosophes* propose. The other's well-being is never a concern for the Sadean subject. Quite the contrary, he or she is propelled by a complete and utter dedication to the propagation of evil: he or she chooses to welter in crime, murder, and revenge. Leo Bersani has forged an interpretation of Sade that intersects my own. He uses the term *imitative sympathy,* which is characteristic of sadism:

Sade's sadism is consistent with the theories of benevolent sympathy which he scornfully rejects. For what Sade rejects is not the mechanism of sympathetic projection assumed by theories of benevolence, but rather the pious view that we are stirred by *virtuous* identifications with others. Virtue is irrelevant to the agitation induced by the suffering of others. It is the identification itself—that is, a fantasmatic introjection of the other—which appears to be intrinsically sexual.[8]

Bersani goes on to say that "there is a certain risk in all sympathetic projections: the pleasure that accompanies them promotes a secret attachment to scenes of suffering or violence."[9] The spectacle of crime must wrest the libertine away from himself; it must be capable of mesmerizing him. And thus Noirceuil tells us: "The degree of violence by which one is moved alone characterizes the essence of pleasure."[10]

Nevertheless, it is wrong to assume that libertines remain unaffected by mimesis; they, too, are creatures of comparison and are continually drawn to imitate and copy each other. (Imitate me! is the motto they invoke as each vies to outdo the others.) Imitation can even be considered, according to Sade, as an aberrant aspect of the libertines' mental behavior, a trait that mobilizes all their sensory data: "The libertine cannot see or hear anything without wanting to imitate it at once."[11] The idea of evil must be communicated from one libertine to the next. A similarity of sentiments, an affective convergence with respect to crime, is sought after. Sympathy, at this level, is what allows the victim to move to the rank of partner, no longer serving the other's lust but, rather, sharing in it.

Imitative activities automatically include an element of overmastery. Sadean imitation is never egalitarian; inherent in it, by virtue of the pleasure principle and the principle of progressive cruelty, is a wish to gain the upper hand over the other. Sadean mimesis is by nature a locus of conflict: a commandment from *La nouvelle Justine* admonishes that one must imitate, but at the same time detest; one must copy, but simultaneously curse. Rivalry between the libertines is expressed above all on the bodies of the victims. The libertines' thirst takes a sacrificial twist: the number of victims available to them is practically unlimited in Sade's text. Harems serve as an outlet for the rage of these models of immorality, whereas the orgy mediates this rage by putting it into circulation through all sorts of combinations and permutations. Ideally, the orgy seeks to equalize pleasures—hence its abhorrence of preferences. There is indeed a hierarchy of libertines in Sade, but they often (through a compounding of defaults) constitute their own ideal models. Education among libertines is not hierarchical but rather reversible. In this connection Barthes wrote that "for the libertines, the educative project has another dimension: they arrive at the absolute of libertinage."[12] The pupil also has the option of turning against his or her preceptor: thus, Juliette poisons Clairwil. Emulation persists among libertines, who covet the place of the other: Noirceuil envies Saint-Fond. Although emulation is now negative, its motivation is unchanged; the imitative mechanism remains structurally intact, the better to produce inversions of position.

One of the enigmas of Rousseau's philosophical discourse—the notion of one's "fellow man," expressed in the two terms *prochain* and *semblable*—reappears in Sade's text, this time with an irreparably negative force.[13] What was problematic in Rousseau is here eradicated once and for all. Sade takes up the principle of the natural isolation of human beings, which finds a mouthpiece in Dolmancé and Noirceuil, indeed in all of his great libertines. For Sade, human relations are doomed to perpetuate their unhappiness, to expose their mortal inconsequence. Noirceuil: "This fellow man is nothing to me, there is not the slightest relation between him and me." Man never leaves behind the original state of war. On the contrary, all relations, in combating isolation, reactivate humanity's original hostility. Dolmancé: "Are we not all born solitary, isolated? I say more: are we not come into the world all enemies, the one of the other, all in a state of perpetual and reciprocal warfare?"[14] In Rousseau's view, we can leave this Hobbesian state through peaceful independence, through a contractual brotherhood, or by delegating sovereignty.

Sade, however, systematically denies this bond of fraternity by recalling man's natural despotism and selfishness. The desire for sovereignty rightfully belongs to each and every individual. In his book *Sade My Neighbor*, Pierre Klossowski approaches the problem by pointing out that "the first step to take toward the renaturalization of cruelty will be to deny the reality of the neighbor, to empty the notion of the neighbor of its content."[15] Dolmancé sees the paradox of this negation of the other in relation to the necessity of crime: "What are . . . the bonds that make up for the isolation in which nature has placed us? Where are the ties that ought to establish relations amongst men?"[16] Reciprocity would seem to be inevitable, and Sade assigns its content a negative character. Klossowski casts the dilemma of the Sadean dialectic in the following terms: "For what, in fact, could be more self-contradictory than the break with the other Sade enjoins? For him, the abolition of our duties to others and the exclusion of others from one's sensibility would always be translated into acts which, in order to be violent, require the other. The acts, then, reestablish the reality of the other and of myself."[17] One way out of this negative pact lies in the apathy of the libertine, in his detached mode of finding *jouissance* in his own criminal actions. The only thing left would be the pure ideality of destruction, the transcendence and autonomy of evil. In apathy, *a-patheia*, even that which evoked the specter of the other is suppressed: the other is no longer taken into account in the affective equation.

Laws and Passions

Sade is Montesquieu's diametric opposite. He mentions Montesquieu in *Juliette*, but only to denigrate him as a second-rate philosopher. Sade exposes the idealistic dimension of his contemporary's political science. The idea of justice, for example, is untenable in Sadean politics. It must be replaced with an implacable judicial relativism, with private passions and interests—the very forces that Montesquieu took pains to repress in his attempt to demonstrate the possibility of peaceful cohabitation. Sade homes in on the most precarious point in *The Persian Letters*, where Montesquieu envisions the possibility of humanity without justice, doomed to reciprocal violence (a vision that is quickly repudiated in the name of man's natural sociability):

> We are surrounded by men stronger than ourselves. They could harm us in myriad different ways and three fourths of the time could get away with it unpunished. What a relief to know that in the

hearts of all these men there exists an interior principle that fights in our favor and protects us from their machinations!

Without that principle, we should be in continual dread: we should walk in front of men as before lions and we should never for a second feel secure about our wealth, our honor, or our life. (letter LXXXIII, 166)

Sade is well aware of a deceptive blind spot in Montesquieu's judgment. Montesquieu, in fact, referring in the same letter to a form of justice that lacks any divine point of reference, writes that it would be "a horrible truth that we should have to hide from ourselves." Justice must be guaranteed by an exterior principle, some kind of transcendence, such as God or a similar model. Or, rather, justice should inspire men with a reciprocal mimetic benevolence, which would act as its guarantor: "Even were there to be no God, we should always love justice—that is to say, do our best to resemble that being of whom we have such a beautiful idea, who if he were to exist, would be, of necessity, just. Free though we might be from the yoke of religion, we ought never to be free from that of equity" (LXXXIII, 166). The judicial bond would thus be a product of reciprocal identification with an idea, with a phantasm of benevolence.

Left to their own devices, however, human beings are incapable of justice; they turn into wolves and lions, preying off each other. Couched in these animal metaphors is the prehistory of our own judicial systems; these images of bestiality reflect humanity's effort to project its own violence outside of itself and to deny its own inhumanity. Montesquieu, it is true, no sooner mentions a natural instinct for justice than it becomes a pretext for rivalry among the group. The winner is whoever manages to outdo his neighbor in justice, whoever is better able to display this sentiment in flattering narcissism, in an impression of domination that will set him above the others: "When a man performs a self-examination, what satisfaction for him to realize that he has a just heart! This pleasure, sober as it may be, must delight him. He finds that his being is elevated as much above those without one as he is elevated above tigers and bears" (LXXXIII, 166). Clearly, justice—now far removed from the benevolent mimesis of which it seemed to be a product—has metamorphosed into an obscene competition, turning each individual into an imperfect mirror of the other. Justice becomes a spectacular duel. This simulation of goodness is revealed in all its falsity: it conceals the worst of intentions.

Sade espouses this competitive conception of the mechanism of justice: from the start he relativizes, personalizes, and narcissizes the idea of justice. He makes it into a human structure riddled with selfishness and contradictions, a sublimation of our passions:

> Let us have the courage to tell men that justice is a myth, and that each individual never actually heeds any but his own; let us say so fearlessly. Declaring it to them, and giving them thus to appreciate all the dangers of human existence, our warning enables them to ready a defense and in their turn to forge themselves the weapon of injustice, since only by becoming as unjust, as vicious as everybody else can they hope to elude the traps set by others. (607)

Sade, in fact, revives tribal law, the world of reprisals, an archaic judicial system based on revenge and bloodshed. If he eschews the traditional duel, it is because he rejects the assumption of equality between the partners, because the duel partakes in a code of honor. Sade's text exhibits a certain nostalgia for the fundamentally ritualistic function of justice. His favorite form of vengeance is what might be termed "vengeance through proxy" (an ancestral form of the duel, according to Sade), essentially a sacrificial process that could be said to operate through the interposition of a scapegoat. The interested parties do not participate in the act of vengeance itself but, instead, choose a third person to replace them:

> Our forefathers, far wiser than we, fought by proxy. . . . the professionals who used to fight on behalf of others were generally regarded as vile persons. . . . Going back to the origin of things, we see that, first of all, these champions were merely hired assassins, such as you still meet with in several cities in Spain and Italy, whom the offended man engaged to rid him of his enemy, and that, next, to mitigate the kind of murder this custom seemed to authorize, the accused was allowed to defend himself against the assassin hired to kill him, and to employ an assassin of his own, and send him into the lists. (946–47)

This exceptional case of delegating vengeance should not be seen as a distancing from violence but, on the contrary, as Sade's adherence to a superior, transcendent, theoretical violence, to the ideality of crime.

Sade rejects the *lex talionis* for the same reasons. The law of the talion is a softened version of natural vengeance in which the reciprocity of punishment is left to the person who has been wronged: "Invested with the right to do his own revenging, the oppressed man will proceed with speed, diligence, economy, and certitude to punish his oppressor and none other" (733). The form of talion that Sade rejects is not reciprocal punishment (*poena reciproca*), in which the guilty person suffers the same harm as that which he inflicted, but its arithmetical version, whereby the degree of punishment is calculated to make it equal or proportional to the crime. The intervention of a third party—a legislator or a judge—dissipates the motive of the originating offense. Wrongs carried out as reparation are always deficient in comparison with the original one. The dispute or clash is affected by difference, a deferral entailing a delay in intensity. In the system of the talion, the punishment is denatured, obfuscated by the aspect of quantitative calculation. It merely copies the criminal intention. Condemning the law of the talion, the *Encyclopédie* says that it "imitates" an evil action.[18] It took Sade's perversity to cast the law of the talion as progress with respect to the resolution of private vengeance, so that its very violence is seen as a representation of vengeance.

According to the Sadean ethos, everyone should be granted the privilege of taking justice into his or her own hands. Justice carried out privately by individuals is a guarantee of social peace: the dissuasive effect of violence is greater and more compelling. Sade's argument has an element of the absurd: "My neighbor's passions are infinitely less to be dreaded than the law's injustice, for the passions of that neighbor are held at bay by mine." He gives this example: "Never will Tom be unjust toward Dick when he knows Dick can retaliate instantly" (732). In a note in *Juliette*, Sade proclaims that vengeance "ought to be tasted by him alone and in private whom the deed has outraged" (78). The law is fundamentally iniquitous for Sade because it is capable of error. It administers justice badly. It is a poor substitute for private vengeance. But above all, the law usurps the rights and passions of the individual; it robs him of the spectacle of his own selfishness. All natural forms of justice therefore must be restored. Similarly, when Sade opposes justice as an idle delay that separates the immediate reparation from the offense, he refuses to admit the sacrifice involved in judicial retribution. Justice does indeed defer its effects. And because of this, it moderates, heading off a renewal of direct confrontation and breaking the chain of infinite retaliation. In *On the Genealogy of Morals*, Nietzsche condemns the law for the same reasons. Like Sade, he expresses nostalgia for those "heroic times" when tribal vengeance reigned as the sole form of justice. In contrast, law imposes itself as pure violence, as the castration of individual passions: "Submission to *law:* how the consciences of noble tribes all over the earth resisted the abandonment of vendetta and were loath to bow before the power of the law! 'Law' was for a long time a *vetitum*, an outrage, an innovation; it was characterized by violence—it was violence to which one submitted, feeling ashamed of oneself."[19]

For Sade, evil by definition inheres in human relations; there is no getting around the relentless violence of reciprocity. Vengeance, which comes in many different forms, can express itself in the most eroticized figures: the orgy, for example, makes possible the circulation of vengeance through all sorts of combinations and permutations. The orgy provides a framework for vengeance, a context in which it can be sublimated in the guise of various pleasures. By pluralizing vengeance, the orgy divests it of any origin. Discussing the contract of revenge in Sade, Marcel Hénaff writes: "This exchange is like a *challenge*, glorious and sacrificial dissipation. . . . Thus, the formula 'Do to me what I did to you,' so often repeated during orgies, comes out of this competitive response, out of this wasteful excess that casts the partners into a delirious expenditure of erotic energies and figures."[20] For Roland Barthes, too, revenge is the essential characteristic of the Sadean relation and is indispensable to the erotic combinatorial system: "[It] ensures the immorality of human relationships."[21]

It follows that the function of the legislator—a sacred office for Montesquieu, Rousseau, and Voltaire—is in Sade's view one of utter degradation. Stripped of all his prestige, this supercitizen is no longer exceptional. In *Juliette*, Sade points alternately to the idiocy and the laziness of lawmakers, who "consulted their stupidity alone, were guided by their mean-spiritedness, their narrow interests, and their myopia" (888–89). Arrogating the right to speak against nature, the legislator is inherently despotic. Sade prefers to lead men back to the time before laws, when the obligation of justice was a matter for the individual: "In him Nature put the necessary instincts and energy for that; taking the law into his own hands he will always obtain a speedier, purer, more incisive, stronger-brewed justice than anything to be had in a courtroom" (731–32). What Sade objects to, as we have seen, is the time interposed by legality. When the reparation of wrongs is left to the law, the intensity of the original act is lost in the process. The law is thus condemned to weakness; it will never have the status of a great spontaneous act. In *Philosophy in the Bedroom*, Sade takes this notion even further: "The law, cold and impersonal, is a total stranger to the passions which are able to justify in man the cruel act of murder" (310). The legislators, invented by philosophers in order to guarantee the possible wisdom of the laws, are labeled impostors. Legal artifice has the same appeal as despotic charlatanism: "Lycurgus, Numa, Moses, Jesus Christ, Mohammed, all these great rogues, all these great thought-tyrants, knew how to associate the divinities they fabricated with their own boundless ambition" (300).

What, then, should be the legislators' responsibility, if any? It lies in what Sade calls *insurrection*, which can be understood as a sort of collective, criminal imitation: "The perpetual immoral subversion of the established order" (315), the perpetual motion of the passions. Sade offers his own ceremonies to the republic: all these new rituals would contribute to the emulation of crime. He proposes to institute festivals in which prizes would be awarded only to the most licentious. The republic must become devoted to unmitigated vice; to this end Sade sets up what amount to laboratories of libertine persuasion. His invectives against priests have much in common with Voltaire's on the same subject: priests are crowd manipulators, Pied Pipers with a stranglehold on public opinion. The legislator also plays out all the forces of mimesis, everything that Rousseau condemned in his reform and foresaw as dangerous, such as public opinion, fashion, and collective festivals.

Another concept dear to political theorists, that of *moeurs*, comes under attack by Sade. For Montesquieu and Rousseau, manners and mores—as the set of behaviors, whether spontaneous or acquired over a period of time, exhibited by a group as a whole—were the most representative domain of the social. Manners are always essentially moral for our *philosophes:* they have their own virtues, their own mechanism of restriction, their own hierarchy. All this is threatened the moment Sade takes over the concept. Mores become immoral—more than mere wordplay, the assertion points to a certain truth because, for Sade, all of society must be saturated by debauchery. Hence the need for microsocieties dedicated to crime: looking forward to a state of generalized corruption, they commit their efforts to the revolution, the global insurrection. Jerome, a libertine in *La nouvelle Justine,* says in the chapter on manners that

> the happiest of all societies will necessarily be the most putrid, and that generally in all its sites . . . I insist that one must try everything, abandon oneself up to everything, and always with preference to the most monstrous-seeming misdemeanors, because it is only by extending the sphere of disorders that we will necessarily attain with greater speed the dose of happiness that is promised by these disorders.[22]

Sade's model society will be found in states where all the passions rule, where laws are silent or else contribute to the people's debauchery. These include Sicily, for instance, but especially all those cultures that are closer to natural law, such as Tahiti, Chili, Mindanao, and so forth.

Although he may adhere to the principle of separation between human beings, Sade continually betrays his conception of the "social whole," the total state. His obsession with natural isolation is surpassed by pacts that contradict the primary thesis of isolation. Once gatherings have become possible, there is no choice but to take perverse advantage of them. Rousseau's general will is transmuted into general lust: the nation is governed completely and exclusively by debauchery, by rank contradiction of the law. Parallel to Rousseau's theory of the general will, generalized lust is not the sum of private vices or individual crimes but, rather, a transcendent principle. Sade envisions debauchery as a totality, an autonomous force, an expression of the corrupt nation. General lust is the despotism of debauchery.

Sade has thus perverted Rousseau's idea of community's transparency, of its unity with itself. Unity is no longer founded on the benevolent communication of consciences but, rather, on a shared desire for crime. Immediacy of communication has become the unmediated transmission of debauchery. The moral of Rousseau's festivals—that all may see and love themselves in one another—has acquired a negative charge in Sade. Rousseau's injunction written in reverse, in its exact inversion, is a blueprint for the universal orgy.

The Politics of the Rogue

The concept of property is placed on a new footing by Sade. If, like Rousseau, he condemns usurpation and conceives of it as an original act of violence, the act of reparation that he proposes takes a different direction from Rousseau's. The nonegalitarian state of nature separates the strong from the weak, the haves from the have-nots. The only means the weak have to redress the balance is through theft. What is more, when people steal, they are imitating an originary theft: that of property itself. Theft is the Sadean equivalent of Diderot's parasitism. Indeed, both *philosophes* find support for their theories in nature itself. The animal world thus functions as a truly self-contained chain of food thievery: "Only by constant thefts do animals manage to preserve themselves, only by countless usurpations do they maintain their existences" (*Juliette*, 115).

Sade elaborates an economic theory that embraces effects that are both perverse (theft succeeds in correcting the distribution of wealth) and absurd (theft actually encourages property, as it incites people to conserve their goods). As in parasitism, the principle of restitution or recovery is operative in theft, but in Sade it strays from its natural pattern (*Juliette*, 119). The weak person who steals is divided from his or her being. Through cunning, skill, or force, the weak person imitates the strong one and plays at being the other. The weak siphons off the character of the strong; he doubles him. He becomes different. In a sense, it is not so much the other's object that the thief steals as the other's person. What is stolen, one might say, is the other.

Theft is in flagrant contradiction to the principle of exchange. It is the radical inversion of the gift. The obligation to take supplants the obligation to give back, in an operation of negative reciprocity. Stealing might even be considered a sort of potlatch in reverse: the point is to liquidate the wealth of the other in a flight of manic excess. What is radically negated by Sade's praise of theft is the mimetic prestige of the object. The object becomes prey to everyone's desires. Constantly exposed to kleptomaniacal aggression, it loses its competitive value. The Sadean object is always iniquitous; it is divisive; it creates inequality and difference. Not only that, the stolen object absorbs the violence of desires; to steal an object is to violate it.

Sade consistently upholds the privilege of private interest over public interest. The idea of a social contract is therefore totally impossible. The happiness and *jouissance* of each individual would be usurped by the social contract, which levels the natural hierarchy in its attempt to equalize wealth. The contract does violence to humanity's essential selfishness. The Sadean individual has nothing to gain from the social contract; it would mean sacrificing everything for nothing. The contract would cause the individual to lose his or her natural liberty, "an unlimited right to everything that tempts him and that he can acquire."[23] The impossibility of the contract is reinforced by Sade's references to anthropological discourse. The natural laws of exchange make it impossible to envision a pact as alienating as Rousseau's can be.

Nothing could be more foreign to Sade's idea of nature than gratuitous giving. Every gift that is received brings with it the obligation for reciprocity. "I give unto you in order that I may obtain from you in exchange": this is the vicious principle that lurks beneath the original act of kindness (*Juliette*, 144). Sade's negation of the gratuitous gesture expresses the inevitability of reciprocity, the impossibility of a one-way act of giving that asks nothing in return. This persistent return of revenge, of the talion, is found in the widespread practice of false hospitality. There is nothing virtuous about hospitality; it is the tainted selfishness of peoples. The guest often falls victim to the hosts' savagery—unless he or she can be exploited to serve their purposes. Once again, Sade seeks support for his hypothesis in anthropological findings. He provides a list of cultures that are hostile to hospitality: the Africans of Zanguebar, the inhabitants of the Cycladic islands, the Thracians, the Arabs, the Loango tribes, the people of Kamchatka, the Athenians, the Spartans—"the entire world, in short" (595).

Hospitality works counter to natural inequality. It makes the weak strong; it encourages dependence. But hospitality's greatest crime is that it succumbs to the prejudice of resemblance. It falls prey to the easy comparisons, recognizing the other as "neighbor" or "fellow man." "Does the material or moral similarity obtaining between two bodies entail the necessity that one of these bodies do good to the other?" asks the libertine Minski in *Juliette* (593). For Sade, the only possible response to this question is negative. One must be hostile to the guest; or even better, one must anticipate the guest's hostility and be the first to act.

Sade's view could be characterized as an aberrant, excessive liberalism, in which the individual's private interest is marked by a veritable hysteria. Private vices combine as public vice: such is Sade's new formulation, which in effect eroticizes Mandeville. The energy of vice is immoral, but it is the motor behind our societies. Insurrection is our destiny. It would be irrelevant to ask Sade where his political allegiance lies; he stands on the side of shattered sovereignty, riddled to the core with conflict. His views on the Revolution of 1789: "The equality prescribed by the Revolution is simply the weak man's revenge upon the strong; it's just what we saw in the past, but in reverse; that everyone should have his turn is only meet. And it shall be turnabout again tomorrow, for nothing in Nature is stable and the governments men direct are bound to prove as changeable and ephemeral as they" (*Juliette*, 120). For Sade, citizens are despots. This distinguishes him from Montesquieu, in whose eyes the republic constrains its citizens to obey the law, which transcends the individual. In Sade's view, the individual retains all of his or her potential force. If there is anything transcendent, it is debauchery. When Sade condemns despotism, it is to the extent that the despot usurps the despotism of others and effectively becomes a tyrant, claiming a monopoly on the energy of evil—whereas in his view this right belongs to everyone; this energy must flow freely through the entire community.

All that counts for Sade is the collective sharing of debauchery, the spoiling of a society corrupted through and through by the desire to imitate in tandem with the cult of evil. In this vein, Sade often resorts to metaphors of epidemics, plague, and contagion. If his political reflections are given to anarchy, it is because they partake of a more radical agenda. Sade's ultimate aim is to attack what lies at the very origin of cultural institutions—the family. The rites that are defended by his depraved philosophical imagination include, above all, rites of copulation. Sade rescinds the prohibition on adultery. Women belong to all men; he refuses to make them into objects of rivalry. But incestuous debauchery reveals even more—a passion, a ravishing of origins. If Sade's text gives expression to a rivalry with God, it is located here, in incest, more than in the multiplication of sexual rituals, which are designed to take the imaginary place of religious rites. In the act of incest, the social impulse is cast in its most enigmatic and most destructive role. In an obscene fashion, it lays hold of its own necessity. Republican *philia,* praised by Rousseau in his *Letter to M. d'Alembert on the Theatre,* is pushed by Sade to the giddy extreme of incest, which is simultaneously its logical outcome and original principle: "[Incest] extends family ties and thus intensifies citizens' love for their country. . . . [It] should be the law for any government that bases itself on fraternity."[24]

Sade's entire opus is radically geared to removing the prohibitions that protect our cultures and underlie the social terrain. This endeavor is motivated by his understanding that prohibitions *contain* violence, in both senses of the word: they somehow fetishize violence by denying it and yet perpetuating its memory at the same time. They take the place of violence. Sade's text thus demolishes prohibitions; he sacrifices them at the altar of perversion. Sade desacralizes and overturns everything. But these new rituals, which are charged with making people impure, achieve their maximum efficacy with the sacrifice of the mother, the natural life principle par excellence. The mother, the first term in the reproductive chain, becomes the scapegoat for all inversions. Sade argues eloquently against parricide as a murderous projection that inverts the emulative values (admiration, respect, obedience, debt to one's ancestors).[25] In a catalog of consanguineous vices, Dolmancé enumerates: "Reciprocal hatreds inveterate; children who, even before reaching the age of reason, have never been able to suffer the sight of their fathers" (354). But no crime can equal that which desecrates the mother, or better, which makes a whore of her. In *Philosophy in the Bedroom*, Eugénie's education and the whole spectacle of initiation that accompanies it reach their apogee in the final ritual torturing of Madame de Mistival. The text effects a remarkable exchange of victims: Eugénie having succumbed to immorality as desired and having acquired libertine dignity, the group now unleashes itself on her mother. Everything in Dolmancé's boudoir is prepared to receive the new guest, who will be sacrificed because maternity represents a principle that is foreign to the assembled group—first and foremost, reproduction. She undergoes a sort of erotic quartering, becoming a sort of *diasparagmos*, dismembered, torn into pieces of pleasure. At the end of the orgy, she is infected with syphilis; her difference is defaced by the libertine disease, a venom or "poison" (363). Sade brings about a striking inversion of sacrificial rites: the victim in this case becomes the receptacle of the community's evil seeds. By being soiled thus, she takes on the attributes of the group that inducts her into their ranks. She is henceforth assimilated into the principle of evil. Madame de Mistival falls into a ritual sleep, approaching death, long enough for her to be contaminated with the sickness; she wakes up condemned to monstrosity.

Through the example of incest, Sade leads us into the icy abyss of undifferentiation. Luxuriating in the process, he describes the demise of culture, dragging cultural institutions toward the most advanced states of disintegration. This is what makes Sade so absolutely modern. Our fascination with him lies in the fact that he fantasizes all our impossible dreams of the omnipotence of passion, all of our violent urges for apocalypse.

Nietzsche condensed the philosophical history of the Enlightenment into the twin destinies of Voltaire and Rousseau. According to Nietzsche, the creative force behind Voltaire's work, the primary motor driving him, was the envy he harbored toward Rousseau. It would be possible to link Rousseau and Sade in a similar destiny. To paraphrase Nietzsche once again, we might say that in the eighteenth century Rousseau's strange fate was to be imitated. His exacerbated individuality made him the negative model, the perverse prototype, of the philosopher. Both Sade and Rousseau realized that culture was inevitably heading toward its anguished twilight. Humanity had no choice but to contemplate its impending doom through half-open eyes, so that Rousseau could become their savior-legislator, and Sade the merry witness of humanity's total decay. Rousseau challenges the progress of the Enlightenment; for Sade, the century trails behind its glorious destiny. Sade jolts it with the contagious velocity of vice.

Sade, forever first and last.

Epilogue / In Praise of Peace

To Immanuel Kant's mind, the sense of historical progress stands
in contrast to a negative conception of that same history, a view
of history from a perspective of stagnation—an Abderitism according to which evil is neutralized by good, and vice versa. The
progressist version of history projected by Kant is opposed to this
Sisyphean assumption. In Kant's view, Abderitism is monstrous;
it is nonhistory, nonprogress. Alexis Philonenko, commenting on
The Contest of the Faculties in which Kant elaborates his approach
to history, reminds us that Abderitism is not, strictly speaking, a
"conception integrated into a philosophical system" but, rather,
that it "designates the spectacle offered by the town of Abdera."[1]
I shall begin by citing Philonenko's description of this town
(adapted from Louis Moreri's *Grand dictionnaire historique*):

> The town of Abdera is famous for the plagues that were visited upon
> it at various times. The air was contagious with pestilence and com-
> municated a kind of extraordinary madness to the people; even ani-
> mals that fed in nearby pastures or drank the waters of the Cossinite
> River were overcome with a kind of rage: perhaps these scourges
> gave rise to the Greeks' ironic proverb on the Theiens' new settle-
> ment: Abdera, the lovely colony of the Theiens. . . . It is said that,
> under the reign of Cassander, King of Macedonia, the Abderites

were inundated by a flood of frogs and rats, which forced them to abandon their town for a time; but nothing is more astonishing than the sickness with which they were afflicted under the reign of Lysimachus in Thrace. A certain Archelaüs, a fine actor, had presented Euripides' *Andromeda* in Abdera. This performance, which occurred in the summer, so stirred the imagination of the town's inhabitants, who had been exposed to violent heat spells that season, that upon leaving the theater most were stricken with a raging fever. Its symptoms were unprecedented: those who were affected ran through the streets declaiming entire passages of Euripides in imitation of Archelaüs. This illness, which ended, not before seven days, in a kind of fit, spread from person to person and held sway over the town until the following winter. If we are to believe Ovid, the inhabitants of this town were accustomed on a particular day to consecrating several unfortunate citizens, by stoning them to death, for the health of the rest.[2]

Kant's desire to emancipate humankind is conceived as a reaction against this "manic stupidity." Abderitism represents a moment of childish madness, of infantile insanity. The task of the Enlightenment is to lead humanity toward reason through progressive reforms. Philonenko interprets the commandment in *Was ist Aufklärung?*—"*Sapere aude*"—as enjoining people to "escape from the unfoundedness of Abderitism";[3] "Abderitism, which is gathering so much favor . . . is now no more than a present that must fade away at the prospect of a moral liberty proposed as an end in itself."[4]

The example of Abdera is interesting, not solely as an illustration of sheer absurdity. From an anthropological perspective the story appears as a symptom of something larger. In fact, Abdera represents a society in continual crisis (plagues, scourges, floods). The evils of Abdera exhibit the common characteristic of undifferentiation. The town's form of madness lies in its perpetually renewed tendency for reciprocal contagion. Moreri singles out one of the most remarkable illnesses to affect the town, the fever brought on by the delirious imagination of the populace. The only explanation for this singular crisis is imitation: all the Abderites start imitating the actor Archelaüs. Possessed by his persona, they begin en masse to declaim the verses they have just heard him pronounce. Another phenomenon also becomes evident: the people of Abdera are able to resolve their continual crises through sacrificial acts, by stoning to death some of their fellow citizens. Commentators tend to tone down the significance of this sacrificial episode. Pierre Bayle, in his *Dictionnaire historique et critique*, compares the massacre of these victims to an auto-da-fé.[5] Philonenko writes: "Isn't this the usual practice in societies, which—as long as the majority is well-off—are hardly given to worrying about the less fortunate?"[6] I maintain, however, that sacrifice must be seen instead as a way of attempting to interrupt the process of undifferentiation. Girardian theory finds a telling illustration in the example of Abdera. The crisis takes hold of the community through generalized imitation. Only by resorting to a sacrificial resolution—an arbitrary and aleatory decision to sacrifice some victims—can the Abderites bring an end (if only temporarily) to the disarray of the town.

The mythical status of this text, with its founding force, must be acknowledged. The town of Abdera is plunged into the cyclical repetition of violence, into a religious impasse. What Kant calls its madness is really its internal violence. The citizens of Abdera can escape the sway of violence only by reenacting the gestures of violence. They are entangled in the mimetic relation. The theater is already a manifestation of the crisis that has them in its grip.

It is interesting to see how the myth excuses the Abderites' violence by exteriorizing it somehow, by blaming it on the imagination or, still better, on the sun or on the strange powers of the pastures. Yet, if Abdera is in crisis, the cause should be sought in the delirious desire for identification. Pierre Bayle writes in his article on the town: "I believe that, once their persistent fever had passed, those who had been the first to act out the play in the streets then infected several other patients. Conditions were therefore ripe for the contagion to spread."[7] Bayle adds that epidemics can affect not only bodies but also minds. He cites the propagation of fanaticism or the phenomena of runaway passions, diseases that spread like plagues or spiritual poxes. In the case of Abdera we are faced with an entire society that is insane, unsound.

Kant is the latest in a succession of interpreters who see this myth as the black hole of man's history. Abderites pay the price for the emancipated evolution of the human species toward reason. They are victims of historiography at the hands of Cicero,

Martial, Juvenal, even Moreri himself, who label them fools, idiots, louts, or the like. Pierre Bayle is aware of this general accusation, immortalized by Moreri, who made the madness of the Adberites into a proverb: *abderitica mens.*

By recalling the example of Abdera, Kant shows that humanity progresses only by distancing itself from contagious, childish imitation. The "manic stupidity" or nonsense of the Abderites, which can encompass all the negative forms of imitation, can go all the way to a catastrophic conclusion: permanent violence, the successive reciprocity of stupidities. In his "Idea for a Universal History with a Cosmopolitan Intent," Kant returns to the negative moment of Abderitism, describing human behavior as "folly and childish vanity and often even childish malice and destructiveness."[8]

In "Idea for a Universal History," Kant's aim is to conceive of a history that accords with a plan determined by nature. He alludes with confidence to the glorious possibility of such a history. Kant takes care to qualify the type of divinatory practice that he has in mind: it is not an expression of religion, self-interest, or political inclination but, rather, a purely rational operation and therefore in harmony with the known laws of nature (he fancies himself the Kepler or Newton of history). Kant also writes that "we will leave it to nature to produce the man who is in a position to write [such a history]" (30). But there is no need to look into the near future (to Hegel, for example) to find this man, for this new prophet is none other than Kant himself.

It could be said that, in the "Idea for a Universal History," Kant corrects the exchangist thesis that dominates the Enlightenment. He puts forward the hypothesis of man's unsocial sociability, positing that human nature lives out this contradiction (30–31). It is man's natural instinct to associate himself with others; nevertheless, in this very movement toward the other, there is a resistance, in favor of his jealously guarded isolation. Sociability is simply impossible to conceive without its opposite. Kant cannot envision the viability of a state of nature like Rousseau's. The period of isolation promotes harmony, but it can make man "eternally dormant" (32).

Man is thus pushed outside of himself, toward culture, toward the other-as-obstacle. And now comes the new period of discord and its inevitable parade of evils. Confrontation with the other leads to inescapable conflict: envy, emulation, and competition fuel discord. But in his fundamental liberalism, Kant thinks that the universal antagonism that pits individual freedoms against each other leads to the good of the greatest number. This superior transcendence absorbs the general resistance and converts it into progress for humanity as a whole: "Thus, thanks be to nature for the incompatibility, for the distasteful, competitive vanity, for the insatiable desire to possess and also to rule" (32).

Such is the artifice of nature, unbeknownst to man. Kant offers the example of the forest. Reciprocal competition between the trees results in beauty:

> It is just as with trees in a forest, which need each other, for in seeking to take the air and sunlight from the others, each obtains a beautiful, straight shape, while those that grow in freedom and separate from one another branch out randomly, and are stunted, bent, and twisted. All the culture and art that adorn mankind, as well as the most beautiful social order, are fruits of unsociableness. (33)

A similar kind of blossoming produces morality, which is a balance between antagonistic gestures of sociability and unsociability. Morality—the effort made in reaction to the other's resistance, in the face of the other's freedom—is a triumph over the savagery of man.

Ships and Camels

Kant is quick to take this notion one step further: what applies to humankind also applies to states. Kant forces us to consider rivalry between nations. His version of peace is conceivable only if we accept from the outset the premise of antagonism and incompatibility between societies.[9] Kant's vision is above all else a "cosmopolitan state in which the security of nations is publicly acknowledged" (36). This utopian association of states does not lose sight of the fragile nature of power relations. The association is envisioned as a way of exerting control over human actions and reactions; its role is to ward off potential conflicts. In this context Kant sees war as the greatest of monstrosities. He cites a passage of Hume in which the Scottish philosopher describes the catastrophic path to which rivalry and violent reciprocity lead: "If, at the present time, I see the nations on the point of war with one another, it is as if I were seeing two besotted fellows beating each other about with cudgels in a china shop. For not only do they have to recover slowly from the bruises they administered to each other, but afterwards they must pay for the damages that they have done."[10] War, as a generalization of the discord between two individuals, is a purely negative energy. It is stupidity, fundamentally contrary to all progress.

How then are we to conceive of eternal peace in the face of such discord? Kant turns to the Abbé de Saint Pierre for his "enthusiasm."[11] In his essay "Perpetual Peace," a treatise on communication, Kant devotes himself to building bridges; he is horrified by the gaps of space that keep groups of men apart: "Uninhabitable parts of this surface—the sea and deserts—separate these communities, and yet ships and camels (the *ship* of the desert) make it possible to approach one another across these unowned regions, and the right to the *earth's surface* that belongs in common to the totality of men makes commerce possible."[12] Kant's version of natural law is friendly, hospitable: it is a matter of converting general hostility into universal hospitality. Hospitality is an apprenticeship in diversity; it transcends local discord (languages, religions, all the elements of chance that separate human beings). Hospitality aims for harmony, understood as an equilibrium among the forces of diversity. From a theoretical perspective, Kant evokes the finite nature of the earth as imposing the inevitability of universal peace. Because we share the planet with one another, we are called on to pull together and to overcome our self-serving acts of violence. In his *Metaphysics of Morals*, Kant adds to what he has said:

> Through the spherical shape of the planet they inhabit (*globus terraqueus*), nature has confined [humanity] within an area of definite limits. Accordingly, the only conceivable way that anyone can possess habitable land on earth is by possessing a part within a determinate whole in which everyone has an original right to share. Thus all nations are *originally* members of a community of the land. . . . It is a community of reciprocal action (*commercium*), which is physically possible, and each member of it accordingly has constant relations with all the others.[13]

From a practical point of view, Kant belongs to the Enlightenment thinkers. He is at home with Montesquieu and Voltaire, who also believed that commerce was an ideal strategy to ensure peace. Montesquieu envisioned commerce as that which in the modern world had to take up where ancient hospitality left off. In *The Spirit of the Laws*, commerce is admitted because it creates interdependence between nations. A single statement is sufficient to convey Montesquieu's thought on the subject: "The history of commerce is that of the communication of people."[14] People come to realize that they share the same desires. They identify with each other in recognizing the convergence of their needs and passions. These exchanges can certainly lead to violence, but as the Enlightenment *philosophes* would have it, only economics allows human beings to manage the objects of rivalry peacefully. Commerce seeks to deny confrontation; it inaugurates forms of reciprocity that are cognizant of the violence inherent in human relations; it is enlightened. Commerce deflects human violence toward the objects of the world, thus averting the possibility that people will take each other as objects of conflict—the threat represented by the Abderites. Direct identification is averted. Mimesis, diverted onto things, is absorbed into competitive acquisition of objects.[15]

Peace requires a true sacrifice. Yet the necessity for a certain moral transcendence brings the *philosophes* back to the religious. Reason would put paid to the notion of original violence, which it attempts to relegate to the oblivion of myth, but reason itself hides a lining of prophecy. Montesquieu's laws are inspired. Voltaire mimes the priest, and Rousseau does the same. Kant writes a science of history, but he ends up assuming a godly posture. The Enlightenment, confronted by the evil of politics, goes down in a display of true religious pageantry, showing that morality cannot be conceived without the guarantee of some sort of transcendence.[16]

Are human beings really incapable of setting limits to their own violence? Will we ever be able to convert original violence into peaceful coexistence, to transform Hobbes's war into a passion for peace? In response to this urgent need, I would suggest the following by way of conclusion: a will to hospitality and respectful identification with the other. Reflecting at the close of *The Gift* on the violent birth of our economies, on the proximity of commerce to war, Marcel Mauss saw that the future of our modern societies depended on averting dangerous encounters and antagonistic, potentially explosive rivalries. In Mauss's view, the will to peace requires a renewed apprenticeship to a particular form of knowledge: people must learn "how to oppose and to give to one another without sacrificing themselves to one another." Reciprocal generosity must take the place of "sordid envy."[17] Let us dispense with prophetic arrogance. Instead of a return to religion, what is called for is a new relation: one of obligation.

Notes

Introduction

1. Ernst Cassirer, *The Philosophy of the Enlightenment*, trans. Fritz C. A. Koelln and James P. Pettegrove (Princeton, N.J.: Princeton University Press, 1951), 234. On this question see also Bronislaw Baczko, "Retour aux origines," in *Rousseau: Solitude et communauté*, trans. Claire Brendhel-Lamhout (Paris: Mouton, Collection "Civilisation et Sociétés," 1974), 60–70.

2. Jacques Derrida, "Force of Law: 'The Mystical Foundation of Authority,'" trans. Mary Quaintance, *Cardozo Law Review* 11.919 (1990): 927, 991.

3. My critique of the Enlightenment remains different from that of Michel Foucault. Following Theodor Adorno and Max Horkheimer, Foucault reads the Enlightenment as a schizophrenic age: on the one hand it wishes to assert human rights, and on the other it establishes a system of inequalities that ravish these very same rights. Foucault sees the contract as fundamentally contradicted by submission, and the universalization of right as contradicted by the disciplinary invalidation of the subject. See Michel Foucault, *Discipline and Punish: The Birth of the Prison*, trans. Alan Sheridan (New York: Pantheon Books, 1977).

I would also distance myself from the Machiavellianism of the *philosophes* referred to by Allan Bloom, our caricatural apostle of the Enlightenment. His version is utilitarian in essence and vulgar: "It was not by forgetting about the evil in man that they hoped to better his lot but by giving way to it rather than opposing it, by lowering standards. The very qualified rationality that they expected was founded self-consciously on encouraging the greatest of all rationalities." See Allan Bloom, *The Closing of the American Mind* (New York: Simon and Schuster, 1987), 291. The evil conceived of by Bloom inevitably leads to good. His principle of evil, freed of its irreducibility, has gained the prestige of use-value.

4. Adam Ferguson, *An Essay on the History of Civil Society* (New Brunswick, N.J.: Transaction Books, 1980), section 4, 20.

5. Simon-Nicolas-Henri Linguet, *Théorie des lois civiles* (Paris: Fayard, 1984), 127.

6. For Marcel Gauchet, this very structure of autonomy is inconceivable. Equality does not necessarily engender harmony. He expresses this convincingly: "Human beings came to recognize themselves through face-to-face opposition. They found the secret of their identity in the very thing that divided them. The same logic, following other paths, will determine their future behavior. Equality, as a continually continued creation, it will not be—that is, everyone the same, everyone in agreement; rather, everyone even more alike, even more akin, in fundamental discord." Marcel Gauchet, *Le désenchantement du monde: Une histoire politique de la religion;* quoted in E. Enriquez, *De la horde à l'Etat* (Paris: Gallimard, 1983).

7. Peter Gay, *The Science of Freedom*, vol. 2 of *The Enlightenment: An Interpretation* (New York: Norton, 1969), 397–447.

8. Act IV, scene 3; cited by Peter Gay, *The Enlightenment*, 2:29.

9. Quoted by Albert Camus in *The Rebel: An Essay on Man in Revolt*, trans. Anthony Bower (New York: Vintage, 1956), 122. Jean-Paul Marat, ideologue of the Terror, did not share Saint-Just's idealism. He writes most decisively on the origins of society that "states owe their origin to violence." Jean-Paul Marat, *Les chaînes de l'esclavage* (Paris: Union Générale de l'Edition, 1972), 40.

10. Carl Schmitt, whose position is closer to my own, is not mistaken. His political philosophy could not be more opposed to that of the Enlightenment; hostility is for him the very stuff of political bonds. He explains with Hobbesian realism: "A relativistic bourgeoisie in a confused Europe searched all sorts of exotic cultures for the purpose of making them an object of its aesthetic consumption. The aristocratic society in France before the Revolution of 1789 sentimentalized 'man who is by nature good' and the virtue of the masses. Tocqueville recounts this situation in words whose shuddering tension arises in him from a specific political pathos: nobody scented the revolution; it is incredible to see the security and unsuspiciousness with which these privileged spoke of goodness, mildness, and innocence of the people when 1793 was already upon them—*spectacle ridicule et terrible.*" Carl Schmitt, *The Concept of the Political*, trans. George Schwab (New Brunswick, N.J.: Rutgers University Press, 1976), 68.

11. "Société," in *Encyclopédie* (Neuchâtel, 1765), 15:252.

12. "Sociabilité," in *Encyclopédie*, 15:251.

13. "Société," in *Encyclopédie*, 15:253.

14. Jean-Jacques Rousseau, "Que l'état de guerre naît de l'état social," in *Ecrits sur l'Abbé de Saint-Pierre*, in *Oeuvres complètes* (Paris: Gallimard, Pléiade, 1964), 3:611.

15. See the introduction to René Girard, *"To Double Business Bound":
Essays on Literature, Mimesis, and Anthropology* (Baltimore: Johns Hopkins University Press, 1978).

16. Pierre Clastres, *Recherches d'anthropologie politique* (Paris: Seuil, 1980), 200.

17. Ibid., 186–87.

18. Claude Lefort, "L'échange et la lutte des hommes," in *Les formes de l'histoire* (Paris: Gallimard, 1978), 22.

19. Jean-Jacques Rousseau, *Emile*, trans. Allan Bloom (New York: Basic Books, 1979), 458.

20. Voltaire, *Dialogues philosophiques* (Paris: Garnier, 1966), 253.

21. Denis Diderot, *Entretiens avec Catherine II*, in *Oeuvres politiques* (Paris: Garnier, 1963), 303–4.

22. Michel Foucault, *The Order of Things: An Archaeology of the Human Sciences*, trans. Alan Sheridan (New York: Pantheon, 1973).

23. Cf. Jürgen Habermas, *Theory of Communicative Action*, trans. Thomas McCarthy (Boston: Beacon Press, 1984).

24. Immanuel Kant, *Annonce de la prochaine conclusion d'un traité de paix perpétuelle en philosophie*, in *Oeuvres philosophiques* (Paris: Gallimard, Pléiade, 1986), 3:420, emphasis added. Immanuel Kant, "To Perpetual Peace: A Philosophical Sketch," in *Perpetual Peace and Other Essays on Politics, History and Morals*, trans. Ted Humphrey (Indianapolis: Hackett, 1983).

25. Reinhart Koselleck, *Critique and Crisis: Enlightenment and the Pathogenesis of Modern Society* (Cambridge, Mass.: MIT Press, 1988), 119.

26. Alexis de Tocqueville, *The Old Regime and the French Revolution*, trans. Stuart Gilbert (Garden City, N.Y.: Doubleday, 1955), 138. Further references will be included parenthetically in the text.

1 / Political Prejudice (Montesquieu)

1. Robert Shackleton, *Montesquieu: A Critical Biography* (Oxford: Oxford University Press, 1961), 316–17; Patrick Riley, *The General Will before Rousseau: The Transformation of the Divine into the Civic* (Princeton, N.J.: Princeton University Press, 1986), 159; Raymond Aron, *Main Currents in Sociological Thought*, trans. Richard Howard and Helen Weaver (New York: Anchor Books, 1965), 1:17.

2. Baron de Montesquieu, *The Spirit of the Laws*, trans. Thomas Nugent, bk. XIX, chap. 12 (New York: Hafner, 1949), 297–98. Further ref-

erences to this work indicating book, chapter, and page number will be provided parenthetically in the text.

3. Montesquieu, "De la politique," in *Oeuvres complètes* (Paris: Gallimard, Pléiade, 1949), 1:114.

4. D'Alembert, *Eloge de Monsieur le Président de Montesquieu*, in Montesquieu, *De l'esprit des lois* (Paris: Garnier-Flammarion, 1967), 78.

5. Quoted by Guy Planty-Bonjour, "L'esprit général d'une nation," in *Hegel et le siècle des Lumières* (Paris: Presses Universitaires de France, 1974), 9. Montesquieu's contemporaries express similar sentiments: the Marquis of Beccaria referred in 1764 to "the great Montesquieu," "the immortal Montesquieu" (Cesare Beccaria, *An Essay on Crimes and Punishments*, [in Italian] [Brookline Village, Mass.: Branden Press, 1983], vii, 2); in 1793 Nicolas Boulanger called him "the Legislator of our century" (Nicolas-Antoine Boulanger, *Recherches sur l'origine du despotisme oriental*, ed. Paul Sadrin [Paris: Les Belles Lettres, 1988], 121).

6. Tzvetan Todorov, *Nous et les autres: La réflexion française sur la diversité humaine* (Paris: Seuil, 1989), 409.

7. Alain Grosrichard, *Structure du sérail* (Paris: Seuil, 1979), 46.

8. Hannah Arendt, *The Human Condition* (Chicago: University of Chicago Press, 1958), 190–91.

9. Louis Althusser, *Montesquieu, Rousseau, Marx: Politics and History*, trans. Ben Brewster (London: Verso, 1982), 61–62.

10. Ibid., 63.

11. Montesquieu, *Oeuvres complètes*, 1:1274.

12. Althusser prefers to speak of the "folly" (*déraison*) of the principle of honor, of its blind madness (*Montesquieu, Rousseau, Marx*, 73).

13. Montesquieu, *The Persian Letters*, ed. and trans. J. Robert Loy (New York: Meridian, 1961), letter XCIX, 187–88. Further citations to this work will provide letter and page numbers in parentheses in the text.

14. Georg Wilhelm Friedrich Hegel, *The Phenomenology of Spirit*, trans. A. V. Miller (Oxford: Clarendon Press, 1977), 311.

15. This "paradox of composition" is treated brilliantly by Jean-Pierre Dupuy in his works on the liberal tradition. See his *Ordres et désordres: Enquêtes sur un nouveau paradigme* (Paris: Seuil, 1982), 167. See also the work on Hume and Mandeville by Dupuy's collaborator Paul Dumouchel, in Paul Dumouchel and Jean-Pierre Dupuy, *L'Enfer des choses: René Girard et la logique de l'économie* (Paris: Seuil, 1979), 211–32.

16. Althusser, *Montesquieu, Rousseau, Marx*, 80.

17. Emile Durkheim, *Montesquieu and Rousseau: Forerunners of Sociology*, trans. Ralph Mannheim (Ann Arbor: University of Michigan Press, 1960), 31–32 (emphasis added).

18. Jean-Pierre Dupuy, *L'Enfer des choses*, 40. Regarding the etymology of the term *envy* (*invitare*: to rival or fight), see also p. 29.

19. Gilles Deleuze and Félix Guattari, *Anti-Oedipus: Capitalism and Schizophrenia*, trans. Robert Harley, Mark Seem, and Helen R. Lane (Minneapolis: University of Minnesota Press, 1983), 194.

20. Montesquieu, *Considerations on the Causes of the Greatness of the Romans and Their Decline,* trans. David Lowenthal (New York: Free Press, 1965), 94.

21. In his study of Montesquieu, Althusser recalled the work of Charles Eisenmann on the separation of powers. *Montesquieu, Rousseau, Marx,* 88–91; see Eisenmann's *"L'Esprit des lois et la séparation des pouvoirs,"* as well as "La pensée constitutionnelle de Montesquieu" in *Cahiers de philosophie politique* 2–3 (1984–85).

22. Montesquieu, *Considerations,* 84.

23. Shackleton, *Montesquieu,* 292.

24. Aron, *Main Currents in Sociological Thought,* 30.

25. Montesquieu, *Considerations,* 93–94.

26. Bernard Manin, "Montesquieu et la politique moderne," *Cahiers de philosophie politique* 2–3 (1984–85): 220.

27. Josué V. Harari, *Scenarios of the Imaginary: Theorizing the French Enlightenment* (Ithaca, N.Y.: Cornell University Press, 1987), 83.

28. See, e.g., Jean Starobinski, "Exile, Satire, Tyranny: Montesquieu's *Persian Letters,"* in his *Blessings in Disguise; or, The Morality of Evil,* trans. Arthur Goldhammer (Cambridge, Mass.: Harvard University Press, 1993), 60–83.

29. Grosrichard, *Structure du sérail,* 158.

30. Suzanne Gearhart, *The Open Boundary of History and Fiction: A Critical Approach to the French Enlightenment* (Princeton, N.J.: Princeton University Press, 1984), 119.

31. See another analysis of this episode in Kevin Newmark, "Leaving Home without It," *Stanford French Review* 11, no. 1 (1987): 17–32.

32. See Luc de Heusch, "The Sacrificial Body of the King," in *Fragments for a History of the Human Body,* ed. Michel Feher, with Rampha Naddaff and Nadia Tazi (New York: Zone, 1989), 387–94.

33. To complete the catastrophe that occurs at the end of *The Persian Letters* and to convey the crisis that Montesquieu describes in its logical perfection, we must add to Roxane's suicide the immolation of the young man who falls into her arms. He, too, is a scapegoat of the new harmony, as Starobinski was the first to remark: "The nameless, almost ghostly youth, who is taken from Roxane's arms and beaten to death by the eunuchs stands for true love, whose part in the drama is shadowy but indispensable and whose immolation leads to the death of the principal characters." Starobinski, *Blessings in Disguise,* 76–77.

34. Jean-Jacques Rousseau, *Discourse on the Origin and Foundations of Inequality among Men,* in *The Basic Political Writings,* ed. and trans. Donald A. Cress (Indianapolis: Hackett, 1987), 79. [Throughout the text Saint-Amand refers to this work as the second *Discourse.* Trans.]

35. This statement has a counterpart relating to the division between the sexes: "There is less communication in a country where each, either as superior or inferior, exercises or is oppressed by arbitrary powers than there is in those where liberty reigns in every station. They do not, there-

fore, so often change their manners and behavior. . . . Their women are commonly confined, and have no influence in society. In other countries, where they have intercourse with men, their desire of pleasing, and the desire men also have of giving them pleasure, produce a continual change of customs" (Montesquieu, *The Spirit of the Laws,* XIX, 12, 298). On Montesquieu's liberalism, see Thomas L. Pangle, *Montesquieu's Philosophy of Liberalism* (Chicago: University of Chicago Press, 1973).

2 / The Spirit of Manners (Voltaire)

1. Voltaire, *The Philosophy of History* (New York: Philosophical Library, 1965), 10. This reprint of the original edition (London, 1766) corresponds to the "Introduction" to Voltaire's *Essai sur les moeurs et l'esprit des nations et sur les principaux faits de l'histoire depuis Charlemagne jusqu'à Louis XIII,* ed. René Pomeau (Paris: Garnier, 1963), 1:3–193. For the rest of the *Essai sur les moeurs,* English-language citations will refer to Voltaire, *General History,* in *The Works of Voltaire,* trans. William F. Fleming (Akron, Ohio: Werner, 1906), vols. 24–30. Where this English translation is incomplete or unsatisfactory, notes will refer to the French edition.

2. Voltaire, *Philosophy of History,* 33, 12.

3. Ibid., 15.

4. Voltaire, "Religion," in *Philosophical Dictionary,* in *The Works of Voltaire,* trans. William F. Fleming (New York: Dingwall-Rock, 1927), 5:76.

5. Ibid.

6. Voltaire, *Philosophy of History,* 40.

7. Voltaire, *Essai sur les moeurs,* 1:340.

8. Ibid., 371.

9. Ibid., 2:804.

10. Georges Benrekassa, *La politique et sa mémoire: Le politique et l'historique dans la pensée des lumières* (Paris: Payot, 1983), 142.

11. Voltaire, *Philosophy of History,* 160.

12. Voltaire, "Prophets," in *Philosophical Dictionary,* 5:27.

13. Voltaire, *Philosophy of History,* 157.

14. Voltaire, *Philosophical Dictionary,* 4:251.

15. Voltaire, *Philosophical Letters,* trans. Ernest Dilworth (New York: Bobbs-Merrill, 1961), 13.

16. Voltaire, *Philosophy of History,* 83.

17. Voltaire, *Essai sur les moeurs,* 2:803.

18. Voltaire, *Philosophy of History,* 245.

19. Ibid., 245–46.

20. Voltaire, *Essai sur les moeurs,* 1:256–57.

21. Voltaire, *Mahomet the Prophet, or Fanaticism: A Tragedy in Five Acts,* trans. Robert L. Myers (New York: Frederick Ungar, 1964), 23.

22. Ibid., 35.

23. Ibid., 12.

24. Hegel, *The Phenomenology of Spirit*, 330.

25. Benrekassa, *La politique et sa mémoire*, 150.

26. Voltaire, *Essai sur les moeurs*, 2:801.

27. Voltaire, *Dictionnaire philosophique* (Paris: Garnier-Flammarion, 1964), 190.

28. Hegel, *The Phenomenology of Spirit*, 330.

29. Ibid., 332.

30. Jean Hyppolite, *Genesis and Structure of Hegel's Phenomenology of Spirit*, trans. Samuel Cherniak and John Heckman (Evanston, Ill.: Northwestern University Press, 1974), 429.

31. Voltaire, *Essai sur les moeurs*, 2:801.

32. Quoted by Benrekassa, *La politique et sa mémoire*, 171.

33. Voltaire, *Philosophical Letters*, 28.

34. Ibid.

35. Voltaire, *Philosophy of History*, 160

36. Ibid., 109.

37. Denis Diderot, *Observations sur le Nakaz*, in *Oeuvres politiques*, ed. Paul Vernière (Paris: Garnier, 1963), 347. And Sade, in his *Philosophy in the Bedroom*, pens this declaration of war on the subject of theocracies: "Let there be no doubt of it: religions are the cradles of despotism: foremost amongst all the despots was a priest: the first king and the first emperor of Rome, Numa and Augustus, associated themselves, the one and the other, with the sacerdotal; Constantine and Clovis were rather abbots than sovereigns; Heliogabalus was priest of the sun. At all times in every century, every age, there has been such a connection between despotism and religion that it is infinitely apparent and demonstrated a thousand times over, that in destroying one, the other must be undermined, for the simple reason that the first will always put the law into the service of the second." The Marquis de Sade, *Philosophy in the Bedroom*, in *Justine, Philosophy in the Bedroom, and Other Writings*, trans. Richard Seaver and Austryn Wainhouse (New York: Grove Weidenfeld, 1965), 305–6.

38. Diderot, *Observations sur le Nakaz*, 346–47.

39. Ibid., 349.

40. René Pomeau, *La religion de Voltaire* (Paris: Nizet, 1969), 111.

41. Quoted by Pomeau, *La religion de Voltaire*, 443.

42. Voltaire, *Philosophy of History*, 166.

43. Sade, *Philosophy in the Bedroom*, 214.

44. Friedrich Nietzsche, *On the Genealogy of Morals*, trans. Walter Kaufmann and R. J. Hollingdale, in *On the Genealogy of Morals and Ecce Homo*, ed. Walter Kaufmann (New York: Vintage, 1967), 115.

45. Voltaire, *Zadig*, trans. H. I. Woolf, in *The Portable Voltaire*, ed. Ben Ray Redman (New York: Viking Penguin, 1977), 329. Further references are given parenthetically in the text.

46. Michel Serres, *The Parasite*, trans. Lawrence R. Schehr (Baltimore: Johns Hopkins University Press, 1982), 44.

47. In the time of the rising bourgeoisie, Voltaire could not have created a creature more consonant with the ideology of the period. Zadig stands in the hypostatized locus of exchange. Everything converges on him. From the "grain of sand" that he was—a nihilistic but potential figure of his desire—he has become a "diamond" (383), a luminous projection of the satisfaction of all and sundry's desires or needs, a fetish, an idol. On the symbolic affirmation of exchange (gold) and desire (the phallus), see Jean-Joseph Goux's *Symbolic Economies: After Marx and Freud*, trans. Jennifer Curtiss Gage (Ithaca, N.Y.: Cornell University Press, 1990).

48. See Suzanne Gearhart, *The Open Boundary of History and Fiction*, 90.

49. See René Girard, *Violence and the Sacred*, trans. Patrick Gregory (Baltimore: Johns Hopkins University Press, 1977).

50. See René Girard's analysis of the sacred-king in *Job, the Victim of His People*, trans. Yvonne Freccero (Stanford, Calif.: Stanford University Press, 1987).

51. René Pomeau is not among those tempted by this error; see his *La politique de Voltaire* (Paris: Colin, 1963), 16.

52. Ever since its publication, Candide's story has been compared to Job's: "He is Job in modern garb!" notes Frederick of Prussia; cited in Jacques van den Heuvel, *Voltaire dans ses contes, de "Micromégas" à "L'Ingénu"* (Paris: Colin, 1967), 259. The *Zadig* narrative borrows quite obviously from the same biblical story. For an excellent reinterpretation of the Book of Job, see Girard, *Job, the Victim of His People*.

53. Voltaire, *Candide*, trans. Richard Aldington, in *The Portable Voltaire*, 229–328. Further references will be provided parenthetically in the text.

54. See Christiane Frémont's powerful analysis of Hobbes in "L'enfer des relations," *Recherches sur le XVIIe siècle* 7 (1984): 69–89.

55. Jacques van den Heuvel is right to point out that "the calamities that the young Westphalian escapes properly affect the multitudes" (*Voltaire dans ses contes*, 257).

56. Patrick Henry believes that we must turn to the story of Job once again for this episode. He examines Candide as a scapegoat, or *pharmakos*, and reminds us that in spite of the playful character of the auto-da-fé episode Voltaire introduces rites and the sacred into culture. See his "Sacred and Profane Gardens in *Candide*," *Studies on Voltaire and the Eighteenth Century* 176 (1979): 148–49.

57. Voltaire, *Philosophical Dictionary*, 5:197.

58. See Jean-Marie Apostolidès, "Le système des échanges dans *Candide*," *Poétique* 48 (November 1981): 449–59. Apostolidès does not, however, perceive the ritualistic dimension of the narrative structure.

59. Michel Foucault, "*Omnes et singulatim*: Vers une critique de la

raison politique," trans. P. E. Dauzat, *Le Débat* (September-November 1986): 15. [Foucault is quoting from Plato's *Politics*. Trans.]

60. Jacques van den Heuvel, *Voltaire dans ses contes*, 279.

61. In this context, see René Girard, "Rite, travail, science" (Rites, work, and science), *Critique* 35, no. 380 (1979): 20–34.

62. Michel Serres, *La naissance de la physique dans le texte de Lucrèce: Fleuves et turbulences* (Paris: Minuit, 1977), 227, 236.

63. Patrick Henry is mistaken, I think, to see in *Candide* traces of a movement from the sacred to the profane, from myth to history; the garden reintroduces the sacred dimension.

3 / The Order of Evils (Rousseau)

1. "They perceived evil, but it was I who discovered its causes," wrote Rousseau in his preface to *Narcisse*. Jean-Jacques Rousseau, *Oeuvres complètes* (Paris: Gallimard, Pléiade), 2:969.

2. Rousseau, *The Confessions*, trans. J. M. Cohen, pt. 2, bk. 8 (Harmondsworth: Penguin Books, 1953), 362.

3. Jean-Jacques Rousseau, *Discourse on the Origin and Foundations of Inequality among Men*, in *The Basic Political Writings*, trans. and ed. Donald A. Cress (Indianapolis: Hackett, 1987), 33. Further references are given parenthetically in the text.

4. Rousseau, *Emile*, 454.

5. In fact, Lévi-Strauss writes in *Tristes tropiques:* "Rousseau, the most ethnographic of the *philosophes:* although he never travelled to distant lands, his documentation was as complete as it could be for a man of his time." Claude Lévi-Strauss, *Tristes tropiques*, trans. John and Doreen Weightman (New York: Atheneum, 1974), 390. See also the chapter in *Structural Anthropology* that is devoted to Rousseau as the founder of ethnology, "Jean-Jacques Rousseau, Founder of the Sciences of Man." Claude Lévi-Strauss, *Structural Anthropology*, trans. Monique Layton (New York: Basic Books, 1976), 2:33–43. An idea of the extraordinary labor that went into Rousseau's work is conveyed by Victor Goldschmidt's monumental book *Anthropologie et politique: Les principes du système de Rousseau* (Paris: Vrin, 1983).

6. Goldschmidt, for example, does not grant imitation the predominant role that it plays in Rousseau's system. Yet it is impossible to conceive of self-love, or pity, without first understanding that they derive from the imitative pattern.

7. Rousseau, *Emile*, 104.

8. Jean-Jacques Rousseau, *Essay on the Origin of Languages*, trans. John H. Moran, in *Two Essays on the Origin of Language*, trans. John H. Moran and Alexander Gode (Chicago: University of Chicago Press, 1966), 46.

9. Ibid., 44–45.

10. Jacques Derrida, *Of Grammatology*, trans. Gayatri Chakravorty Spivak (Baltimore: Johns Hopkins University Press, 1974).

11. Rousseau, *Essay on the Origin of Languages*, 13.

12. Derrida, *Of Grammatology*, 277.

13. Jean-Jacques Rousseau, *Rousseau, Judge of Jean-Jacques: Dialogues*, trans. Judith R. Bush, Christopher Kelly, and Roger D. Masters, in *The Collected Writings of Rousseau*, ed. Roger D. Masters and Christopher Kelly (Hanover, N.H.: University Press of New England, 1989), 1:153.

14. In the *Supplement to Bougainville's "Voyage,"* Diderot will later emphasize the mimetic quality of the gesture of possession, which effects a multiplication of doubles: "All warfare originates in conflicting claims to the same bit of property. The civilized man has a claim which conflicts with the claim of another civilized man to the possession of a field of which they occupy respectively the two ends, so the field becomes the object of a dispute between them." Denis Diderot, *Supplement to Bougainville's "Voyage,"* trans. J. Barzun and R. H. Bowen (Indianapolis: Bobbs-Merrill, 1983), 184.

15. Derrida, *Of Grammatology*, 190.

16. Rousseau, *Rousseau, Judge of Jean-Jacques*, in *Collected Writings*, first dialogue, 1:9. In his masterly analysis of the Social Contract, Lucien Scubla sees this definition of desire as a prefiguration of Girardianism. See "Sur l'impossibilité de la volonté générale chez Rousseau," *Cahiers du C.R.E.A.* 1 (1982). Sympathy, Adam Smith's variant of pity in his *Theory of Moral Sentiments*, first published in 1759, also contains all the ambivalence of self-love (*amour-propre*). Jean-Pierre Dupuy writes: "We are constantly putting ourselves in the place of others in thought, but in reality, we never leave our own . . . the subject in Smith is irremediably trapped within the world of his own sensibility." See Jean-Pierre Dupuy, "De l'émancipation de l'économie: Retour sur 'le probleè d'Adam Smith,'" in *L'Année sociologique*, 37 (1987): 311–42.

17. Jean Starobinski, *Jean-Jacques Rousseau: Transparency and Obstruction*, trans. Arthur Goldhammer (Chicago: University of Chicago Press, 1988). Starobinski discusses Rousseau's use of the word in some detail, 218–24.

18. Rousseau, *Judge of Jean-Jacques*, first dialogue, 1:9.

19. Rousseau, *Emile*, 221.

20. Rousseau, *Essay on the Origin of Languages*, 32.

21. Jean-Jacques Rousseau, *Politics and the Arts: Letter to M. d'Alembert on the Theatre*, trans. Allan Bloom (Glencoe, Ill.: Free Press, 1960), 18. Further references are given parenthetically in the text.

22. Jean-Jacques Rousseau, "Lettre de J. J. Rousseau à Monsieur Philopholis," in *Oeuvres complètes*, 3:236.

23. Theater fills Rousseau with terror. What horrifies him about theatrical imitation is the magic of the double that the theater capitalizes on. Whence the famous distinction that Rousseau makes between the orator and the actor: the orator speaks in his own name, while the actor

effaces himself in the role of another. Rousseau's almost superstitious horror is revealed in his narration of this memory of reading: "I read when I was young, a tragedy, which was part of the Escaplade, in which the Devil was actually one of the actors. I have been told that when this play was once performed, this character, as he came on stage, appeared double as if the original had been jealous that they had had the audacity to imitate him, and instantly everybody, seized by fright, took flight, thus ending the performance." Rousseau, *Letter to M. d'Alembert on the Theatre,* 121.

Isn't it the devil's peculiar property precisely that of doubling himself, of being enthralled by his own imitation? This story seems to be emblematic of everything that Rousseau holds against the theater: the diabolical fermentation of the art, its infinite power of illusion, its ability to surpass itself in multiplying masks. What Rousseau's reminiscence stages so admirably or, rather, what it theorizes, is the conflict between the copy and the original. In other words, mimesis itself becomes rivalrous. In the end Rousseau establishes, through the very movement of imitation, a chain of reversible doublings. Such a crisis of difference can be resolved only by a flight into panic; otherwise, representation itself becomes untenable and must be banished.

24. Jean-Jacques Rousseau, *The Government of Poland,* trans. Willmoore Kendall (Indianapolis: Hackett, 1985), 15.

25. Rousseau, *The Government of Poland,* 14–15.

26. René Girard, *Things Hidden since the Foundation of the World,* with Jean Michel Oughourlian and Guy Lefort, trans. Stephen Bann and Michael Metteer (Stanford, Calif.: Stanford University Press, 1987), 20.

27. Jean-Jacques Rousseau, *La nouvelle Héloïse* (Paris: Garnier-Flammarion, 1967), 607.

28. Ibid., 608.

29. Ibid., 610–11.

30. In *Of Grammatology,* Derrida rather summarily asserts that Rousseau's festivals take place without "sacrifice, without expense, and without play" (307). In the same analysis, however, he says that the "festival represses the relationship with death." The entire, visible order of the festival is designed, on the contrary, to contain the risk of unhappiness.

31. These actors are also the only kind who are worthy of the city, as this is the only good kind of political comedy. In a remark in the letter that Rousseau himself acknowledged as extreme, the horrified author predicted that the domain of politics would be invaded by the world of theater: "The elections will take place in the actresses' dressing rooms, and the leaders of a free people will be the creatures of a band of histrions" (123).

32. Starobinski also stumbles over the difficulty of this passage, whose mystery he emphasizes: "*Nothingness* (as to the object of representation) is strangely necessary if subjective *totality* is to emerge." *Transparency and Obstruction,* 96. The disappearance of the object, he finds, indicates

the suppression of evil as mediation. One could put it better by saying that the object is sacrificed (hence its strange present-absent status); its disappearance is the scapegoat that makes possible the group's harmony. It is in terms of sacrifice that we must read the anecdote involving the ritual stake, which Rousseau proposes as an invitation to congregate: "Plant a stake crowned with flowers in the middle of a square; gather the people together there, and you will have a festival." *Letter to M. d'Alembert*, 126.

33. Robert Derathé, Introduction to Rousseau, *Du contrat social*, in *Oeuvres complètes*, 3:xcii, xciii.

34. Rousseau, *On the Social Contract, or Principles of Political Right*, in Jean-Jacques Rousseau, *The Basic Political Writings*, trans. and ed. Donald A. Cress (Indianapolis: Hackett, 1987), 157. Further references are given parenthetically in the text.

35. Louis Althusser, *Montesquieu, Rousseau, Marx*, 144.

36. Rousseau, *La nouvelle Héloïse*, 547–48.

37. Althusser, *Montesquieu, Rousseau, Marx*, 120.

38. When Rousseau criticizes monarchical government, it is because it stands the furthest from the general will. Monarchy is in fact the most obvious example of an individual will: "There are no opposing movements which are at cross purposes with one another" (*Social Contract*, 183). Opposing powers would be especially desirable in this case. The immobility that characterizes monarchy is proof of the people's unhappiness.

39. See Rousseau, *Fragments politiques*, in *Oeuvres complètes*, 3:536 (fragment XI, "De la patrie").

40. This chapter of Rousseau's text bears strong similarities to Voltaire's *Essai sur les moeurs*.

41. Starobinski, *Transparency and Obstruction*, 288.

42. Michel Serres, *Le parasite* (Paris: Grasset, 1980), 161.

43. Benrekassa, *La politique et sa mémoire*, 113.

44. Rousseau's arrogance will prompt him to claim this mythic role for himself, even if he does so facetiously: "For since I am a direct descendent of these princes [Rousseau has named King Adam and Emperor Noah], and perhaps of the eldest branch, how am I to know whether, after the verification of titles, I might not find myself the legitimate king of the human race?" Rousseau, *Social Contract*, 143.

45. In *Emile*, Rousseau writes: "The necessary relations between morals and governments have been so well expounded in the book *The Spirit of the Laws* that one can do no better than have recourse to this work to study these relations." Rousseau, *Emile*, 468.

46. Rousseau, preface to *Narcisse*, in *Oeuvres complètes*, 2:971.

47. Rousseau, *The Government of Poland*, 8.

48. Ibid., 6. In his study *Moses and Monotheism* Freud explains the prophet's mission as an idealization of spirituality. The Jewish nation benefited from a heightened consciousness of itself; it felt superior to the

peoples who remained under the hold of the senses. In the section titled "The Progress in Spirituality," Freud discusses the parallel between the Jews' belief in being the chosen people and the dematerialization of God. Sigmund Freud, *Moses and Monotheism*, trans. Katherine Jones (New York: Vintage, 1955), 142–47.

49. Rousseau, *The Government of Poland*, 7.

50. Ibid., 69, 73.

51. Rousseau, *Projet de constitution pour la Corse*, in *Oeuvres complètes*, 3:921.

52. Rousseau, *The Government of Poland*, 72.

53. Ibid.

54. Ibid., 96.

55. Ibid., 16.

56. Ibid., 4.

57. Ibid., 21.

58. Ibid., 23.

59. Rousseau will also add to the polemics against superstition that raged among the *philosophes* during this period. Nevertheless, he does not substitute reason for faith but, rather, supports patriotic devotion in the place of religious faith. He proposes this new religion for the Corsicans: "We would divert them from superstition by keeping them well occupied with their duties as citizens; by adding pomp to national festivities, by taking much of their time away from church ceremonies and devoting it to civil ceremonies." Rousseau, *Projet de constitution pour la Corse*, in *Oeuvres complètes*, 3:944.

60. Rousseau, *Projet de constitution pour la Corse*, in *Oeuvres complètes*, 3:913.

61. Rousseau, *The Government of Poland*, 74.

62. Serres, *The Parasite*, 150.

63. Rousseau, *Fragments politiques*, in *Oeuvres complètes*, 3:526 (fragment VIII, "Economie et finances").

64. Rousseau, preface to *Narcisse*, in *Oeuvres complètes*, 2:964.

65. When Rousseau speaks out against the cooperative exchange of skills, he is recalling ritual constraints; he feels compelled to do away with religious obligation. See *Discourse on the Origin of Inequality*, 65–67.

66. Rousseau, *Essay on the Origin of Languages*, 37.

67. See Althusser, *Montesquieu, Rousseau, Marx*, 158–59.

68. Rousseau, *La nouvelle Héloïse*, 414.

69. Ibid., 418.

70. Rousseau, *Projet de constitution pour la Corse*, in *Oeuvres complètes*, 3:912.

71. Rousseau, *Emile*, 468.

72. Rousseau, *Projet de constitution pour la Corse*, in *Oeuvres complètes*, 3: 914.

73. Starobinski, *Transparency and Obstruction*, 103.

74. Rousseau, *The Reveries of the Solitary Walker*, trans. Charles E. Butterworth (New York: New York University Press, 1979), 82.

75. Ibid.

4 / Taking Positions (Diderot)

1. Denis Diderot, *Rameau's Nephew and Other Works*, trans. Jacques Barzun and Ralph H. Bowen (Indianapolis: Bobbs-Merrill, 1956), 50. Further citations will appear parenthetically in the text; in a few cases, where a new translation has been made, notes refer to the French text.

2. Derrida, *Of Grammatology*, 205.

3. Serres, *The Parasite*, 230.

4. Cited in Abbé Raynal, *Des peuples et des gouvernements* (Paris: Bobée, 1822), 101.

5. [Diderot uses the term *aliénation*. *Le neveu de Rameau* (Paris: Flammarion, 1983), 109. Trans.]

6. Serres, *The Parasite*, 192.

7. Ibid.

8. The king, of course, is the main piece in chess. Literature on the game tells us that the origin of the expression *checkmate* (from the Old French *eschec mat*) is the Persian expression *shah mat*, meaning "the king is dead." In the *Encyclopédie* article (*"Echecs"* [Chess]) by the Chevalier Jaucourt, he informs us that the term means "the king is taken." Chess, according to the Persian etymology, would mean the game of the king.

9. Girard, *Violence and the Sacred*, 253.

10. On the duality of the king and how he is doubled as his own victim in the character of his jester, René Girard points out the analysis of Shakespeare's *Richard II* in Ernst H. Kantorowicz's *The King's Two Bodies: A Study in Medieval Political Theology*. See Girard, *Violence and the Sacred*, 305.

11. *Encyclopédie*, 12:510.

12. Ibid.

13. Rousseau, *Discourse on the Origin of Inequality*, 64.

14. Freud commented on Diderot's intuition of the oedipal scenario; see *A General Introduction to Psychoanalysis*, rev. ed., trans. Joan Riviere (New York: Washington Square Press, 1952), 346.

15. Girard, *Violence and the Sacred*, 188.

16. Ibid.

17. Diderot, *Le neveu de Rameau*, 116.

18. Girard, *Violence and the Sacred*, 71.

19. Ibid., 62.

20. Michel Serres reminds us that the term *satura* is used to designate the "strategy of amalgamation in political matters, or a block vote on

diverse laws." See Michel Serres, *Rome: The Book of Foundations*, trans. Felicia McCarren (Stanford, Calif.: Stanford University Press, 1991), 202.

21. Jean-Claude Bonnet, Introduction to *Le neveu de Rameau*, 21.

22. Ibid., 25.

23. In his essay *The Gift*, Marcel Mauss explicitly shrouds the countergift in negative values. The gift given in return bears the invidious stamp of rivalry: it always conveys the desire to outdo the giver, to one-up or overtake him, to get one's revenge. Mauss writes that "we still feel the need to *revanchieren*, as the Germans say." Marcel Mauss, *The Gift: The Form and Reason for Exchange in Archaic Societies*, trans. W. D. Halls (London: Routledge, 1990), 7.

24. An ironic effect that also reaches Diderot's enemies: when at the close of his career Palissot wrote *L'homme dangereux*, a satire on the "slander-mongers," the public thought that it was addressed to Palissot himself. See Jean-Claude Bonnet, "Dossier," *Le neveu de Rameau*, 190.

25. Diderot, "Encyclopédie," in *Encyclopédie*, 5:648a.

26. Ibid., 636 (Diderot's emphasis).

27. Denis Diderot, *Observations sur le Nakaz*, in *Oeuvres politiques*, ed. Paul Vernière (Paris: Garnier, 1963), 401.

28. Diderot, *Le neveu de Rameau*, 112.

29. Denis Diderot, *Entretiens avec Catherine II*, in *Oeuvres politiques*, 303.

30. Jacques Chouillet, "Les machines de Diderot (écrits politiques)," *Revue des sciences humaines* 58, nos. 186–187 (April-October 1982–83): 257–65.

31. Diderot, *Observations sur le Nakaz*, 359.

32. Diderot, *Entretiens avec Catherine II*, 305.

33. Ibid., 306.

34. Diderot, *Essais sur la peinture*, in *Oeuvres esthétiques*, ed. Paul Vernière (Paris: Garnier, 1968), 713.

35. Jean Starobinski, "Action et réaction chez Diderot," in *Dilemmes du roman* (Saratoga, Calif.: Anma Libri, 1989), 78–79.

36. Diderot, *Observations sur le Nakaz*, 378–79.

37. Diderot, *Entretiens avec Catherine II*, 307.

38. Diderot, *Observations sur le Nakaz*, 421.

39. Rousseau, *Discourse on the Origin of Inequality*, 99.

40. *Supplement to Bougainville's "Voyage,"* in Diderot, *Rameau's Nephew and Other Works*, 181. Further references to this text will be given parenthetically.

41. Rousseau, *Fragments politiques*, in *Oeuvres complètes*, 3:535–36.

42. Rousseau, *Discourse on the Origin of Inequality*, 99.

43. Denis Diderot, *D'Alembert's Dream*, in *Rameau's Nephew and Other Works*, 124.

44. Rousseau, *Emile* (Paris: Garnier-Flammarion, 1966), 38–39.

45. Denis Diderot, "Hobbisme," in David Hobbes, *Le citoyen* (Paris: Garnier-Flammarion, 1982), 404.

5 / The Politics of Crime (Sade)

1. Following Barthes here, I "include in this word . . . all torture and debauchery." Roland Barthes, *Sade, Fourier, Loyola,* trans. Richard Miller (Berkeley and Los Angeles: University of California Press, 1989), 15.

2. Marquis de Sade, *Juliette,* trans. Austryn Wainhouse (New York: Grove Press, 1968), 888. Further references to this translation will appear parenthetically in the text. Notes will refer to the French edition.

3. Marquis de Sade, *Histoire de Juliette,* in *Oeuvres complètes* (Paris: Pauvert, 1987), 8:160.

4. Albert Camus perceived this clearly when he remarked that unlimited freedom of desire, inasmuch as it negates the other, necessitates the suppression of pity. See *The Rebel,* 42.

5. Barthes, *Sade, Fourier, Loyola,* 23–24.

6. See Marcel Hénaff, *Sade, l'invention du corps libertin* (Paris: PUF, 1978), 198–99. Hénaff also refers to the libertines' wasteful indulgence in comparison as a kind of potlatch. The idea of potlatch, however, includes more than just lavish squandering, luxurious expenditure, glorious loss. In his essay on the gift, Marcel Mauss locates a "principle of rivalry" at the heart of the practice of potlatch. He views these gifts as "exchanges comprising very acute rivalry," of unrestrained emulation. Mauss, *The Gift,* 6, 7.

In his analysis of Mauss, Claude Lefort points out that the potlatch is a face-to-face encounter with the other. What is sought after in this type of giving is recognition by others. For Lefort, the squandering or destruction of the object has precisely this value. Lefort mentions that the Haida Indians say that they "kill" wealth. One could say that squandering is a kind of sacrifice; it is the price of warring confrontation with the other. See Lefort, "L'échange et la lutte des hommes," in *Les Formes de l'histoire,* 15–29.

7. Rousseau, *Discourse on the Origin of Inequality,* 55.

8. Leo Bersani, "Represention and Its Discontents," in *Allegory and Represention,* ed. Stephen Greenblatt (Baltimore: Johns Hopkins University Press, 1981), 150.

9. Ibid.

10. Sade, *Histoire de Juliette,* 8:183.

11. Marquis de Sade, *The 120 Days of Sodom and Other Writings,* trans. Austryn Wainhouse and Richard Seaver (New York: Grove Press, 1966); quoted by Bersani, "Representation and Its Discontents," 145.

12. Barthes, *Sade, Fourier, Loyola,* 24.

13. [In French the two terms *prochain* and *semblable* designate one's fellow man: the first, sometimes rendered as "neighbor," denotes "someone who is in close proximity"; the second denotes "one who is similar." Trans.]

14. *The Complete Justine, Philosophy in the Bedroom, and Other Writings,* trans. R. Seaver and A. Wainhouse (New York: Grove Press, 1965),

283–84. Further references to *Philosophy in the Bedroom* will be included parenthetically in the text. Where this translation is inadequate, notes will refer to the French edition.

15. Pierre Klossowski, *Sade My Neighbor*, trans. Alphonso Lingis (Evanston, Ill.: Northwestern University Press, 1991), 91.

16. Sade, *La philosophie dans le boudoir* (Paris: Union Générale des Editions, 1972), 177–78.

17. Klossowski, *Sade My Neighbor*, 96.

18. "Talion," in *Encyclopédie* 15:864. For Marc Guillaume, the law of the talion is essentially a kind of epidemic, a principle of circulations and sequences. See Guillaume, *La contagion des passions* (Paris: Plon, 1989), 119.

19. Nietzsche, *On the Genealogy of Morals*, third essay, section 9, 114.

20. Hénaff, *Sade, l'invention du corps libertin*, 256.

21. Barthes, *Sade, Fourier, Loyola*, 165.

22. Sade, *La nouvelle Justine*, in *Oeuvres complètes*, 7:34–35.

23. Rousseau, *On the Social Contract*, 151.

24. Sade, *La philosophie dans le boudoir*, 241–42.

25. See, for example, Saint-Fond's long diatribe on parricide in *Juliette*, 252–54.

Epilogue / In Praise of Peace

1. Alexis Philonenko, *La théorie kantienne de l'histoire* (Paris: Vrin, 1986), 47.

2. Ibid., 47–48. Philonenko's source is Louis Moreri, *Grand diction-naire historique, ou le mélange curieux de l'histoire sacrée et profane* (Paris: J.-B. Coignard, 1732), 1:22.

3. Immanuel Kant, *Was ist Aufklärung?* in *La philosophie de l'his-toire* (Paris: Denoël-Gonthier, 1947).

4. Philonenko, *La théorie kantienne*, 50–51.

5. Pierre Bayle, "Abdère," *Dictionnaire historique et critique* (Rotter-dam: Reinier Leers, 1702), 1:13.

6. Philonenko, *La théorie kantienne*, 48.

7. Bayle, "Abdère," 12.

8. Immanuel Kant, "Idea for a Universal History with a Cosmopoli-tan Intent," in *Perpetual Peace and Other Essays*, trans. Ted Humphrey, 29–30. Further references will be included parenthetically in the text.

9. As Benrekassa writes, rivalry between nations is the only political model recognized as true in the eighteenth century. See *La politique et sa mémoire*, 219.

10. David Hume, quoted in Immanuel Kant, *The Conflict of the Facul-ties; Der Streit der Fakultäten*, trans. Mary J. Gregor (New York: Abaris Books, 1979), 171. [Gregor's rendering follows the German version used by Kant; Hume's actual words were as follows: "I must confess, when I

see princes and states fighting and quarrelling, amidst their debts, funds, and public mortgages, it always brings to my mind a match of cudgel-playing fought in a china-shop." David Hume, "Of Public Credit," in *Essays, Moral, Political and Literary* (London: Longmans, Green, and Co., 1875), 1:371. Trans.]

11. Writing about the work of the Abbé de Saint Pierre, whom he most likely discovered through reading Rousseau's "Extrait du projet de paix perpetuelle de Monsieur l'Abbé de Saint Pierre": "The greatest minds that have sought to work for the good of humanity have been enthusiasts." Quoted by J. Ferrari, *Les sources françaises de la philosophie de Kant* (Paris: Klincksieck, 1979), 218.

12. Kant, "To Perpetual Peace: A Philosophical Sketch," *Perpetual Peace and Other Essays,* 118.

13. Immanuel Kant, "Métaphysique des moeurs," in *Oeuvres philosophiques,* 3:626.

14. Montesquieu, *The Spirit of the Laws,* book XXI, section 5, 334.

15. As we know, Rousseau's thinking on this question tells quite a different story. For him, commerce between nations originates as a corrupted residue of the natural compassion that men feel for each other. It is a bastardized form, a paler version of original pity; only a few cosmopolitan spirits have held on to this primary sentiment. An "international contract" that Rousseau envisioned as a counterpart to the *Social Contract* never materialized, but given the isolationist policy that he recommended nations follow, the logical possibility of this international contract is questionable.

16. For Albert Camus in *The Rebel,* the Enlightenment effort to found a new judicial system foundered as a new transcendence was sought. Justice took the place of a henceforth absent God. Paraphrasing Camus, one could say that God had to die in the name of the social contract. See the section on "The Regicides" in chap. 3, "Historical Rebellion" (112–32). I have tried to show how law continued to verge on religion. The divine principle aside, what the *philosophes* found somehow inescapable was the whole world of rites, the necessity for a sacred foundation for the social.

17. Mauss, *The Gift,* 82–83.

Index

Compiled by Hassan Melehy

Pierre Saint-Amand is Francis Wayland Professor of French Studies and Comparative Literature at Brown University and the author of, among other books, *Diderot: Le Labyrinthe de la relation* (1984) and *The Libertine's Progress: Seduction in the Eighteenth-Century French Novel* (1994).

Jennifer Curtiss Gage, who earned a Ph.D. in French literature from Brown University, is a professional translator whose published translations include theoretical works by Jean-Joseph Goux, the memoirs of André Weil, and poetry by Philippe Jaccottet, as well as a number of previous works by Pierre Saint-Amand. For her translation of Dominique Rolin's novel, *The Deathday Cake*, she was awarded the Gregory Rabassa Prize by the American Literary Translators Association in 1985. She has also published translations of poetry and essays from the Dutch.

Chantal Mouffe is senior researcher at the Centre for the Study of Democracy at the University of Westminster in London.